ATARI ST
Machine
Language

Complete introduction to machine/assembly
language on the ATARI ST

By B. Grohmann, P. Seidler & H. Slibar

A Data Becker Book

Published by

Abacus Software

Fourth Printing, March 1989
Printed in U.S.A.
Copyright © 1985, 1987, 1988   Data Becker GmbH
    Merowingerstraße 30
    4000 Düsseldorf, West
Germany
Copyright © 1986, 1987, 1988   Abacus Software, Inc.
    5370 52nd Street SE
    Grand Rapids, MI 49508

ISBN   **0-916439-48-8**

Table of Contents

Preface

This book is intended especially for those new to machine language. In general, we assume that you have mastered the fundamentals of a programming language. Since programming in machine language requires a solid knowledge of the construction and operation of a computer, we have included a chapter in this book to present these primary topics.

The chapters presenting the practical examples in machine language take up relatively little room in the book when one considers that they are really our theme. But our purpose is not to offer as many practical examples as possible, but to lead into our theme systematically. To a degree, we have also "developed" our machine language examples for this purpose.

In the final analysis, programming in machine language does not differ in principle from programming in a high-level language. The assembler and microprocessor commands are only much less "powerful" than those of a high-level language. By this we mean that more commands are required to write a program in assembly language than for the equivalent in Logo, for instance. But assembly language programs are faster and can solve problems that are almost impossible in a high-level language.

This book is written especially for the Atari ST; the examples given can be executed on this computer directly. If you use assembly tools for assembly language programming other than those we used, you will have to modify the programs slightly (start address, etc.). The documentation included with your assembler will contain the necessary information. Apart from that, you should execute the examples as TOS applications.

Last, but not least, we would like to thank all of those who helped with the creation of this book and with its corrections, in particular Andreas Lucht, who brought several "oversights" to our attention.

Berlin, August 1985

Bernd Grohmann
Petra Seidler
Harald Slibar

Chapter One

Microcomputer Fundamentals

- •Introduction

- •Representation of data

- •Logical operations and bit manipulation

- •Program creation

Introduction

This chapter will describe the fundamentals of program development. Readers who are familiar with these terms can skim through this section. However, we believe that even the experienced programmer will find some interesting subjects here.

What do we mean by programming?

Given a problem, we must search for a solution. We try to find a step-by-step procedure to solve the problem. This step-by-step procedure is called an algorithm. Often we try to divide the problem into smaller sub-problems that are easy to solve.

An algorithm represents a set of rules by which a problem may be solved step by step. It may consist of only a finite number of steps. The algorithm can be expressed in any desired symbols or language. A simple example of an algorithm is:

> 1) Turn the cassette recorder's power on.
> 2) Insert the cassette.
> 3) Select the desired volume.
> 4) Press the recorder's "play" button.

As soon as a solution to a problem is described as an algorithm, it can be translated into a set of symbols, or a "language" that a computer can understand. English or other "natural" languages are not well-suited to writing programs. The reason for this is that every natural language contains many syntactic ambiguities that the computer cannot understand. An artificial language can be created, however, with all its terms well-defined. The terms can even be borrowed from a natural language in order to make it easier for humans to read and understand. This type of artificial language is called a programming language.

However, the computer usually cannot understand a programming language. The computer knows only a something called machine language. Utility programs are required that take programs written in a programming language and convert them to the machine language of the computer.

It is possible to convert the algorithm directly to machine language. But since the internal representation of the machine language instructions is not very descriptive, something called assembly language is used. Each assembly language instruction represents exactly one machine language instruction. A program called an assembler takes a program written in assembly language and converts it to machine language. The other features of an assembler will be described in the following chapters.

Data Representation

Data is processed in some manner by every program, whether the program interprets or creates it. Therefore data must also be converted to a form that the computer can work with.

Representing numerical data

In order to understand the representation of numerical data in the computer, it makes sense to take a look at the elementary representation of numbers. So, we will first describe the decimal system.

In the decimal system, a number is expressed as a sequence of digits. As the name decimal system implies, there are ten different digits from 0 to 9. Each of these has a specific value depending on the place in the number at which the digit is located. In general, this means that a digit in the "nth" place in the number has ten times the value of a digit in the (n-1)th place. For example, the "1" in the number "1000" has ten times the value of the "1" in the number "0100".

The number "12345" is just an abbreviated notation for the expression:

```
1*10000 + 2*1000 + 3*100 + 4*10 + 5*1
```

or, written "mathematically":

$$1*10^4 + 2*10^3 + 3*10^2 + 4*10^1 + 5*10^0$$

It should be noted that, in the decimal system, the value of a digit is determined by its position. The Roman numeral system , for example, does not conform to this method.

The system of digits and positions has certain advantages when it comes to calculations. Since each place (position) describes a certain range of the number, the calculations can be performed place by place. For example, an addition can be performed as follows:

```
      235
  +   582
  -----------
      817
```

First the right column is added: 5+2=7.

Then the middle column: 3+8=11. This can be thought of as a "1" and a carry of "1".

The carry is added to the two digits in the next column: 2+5 +1=8.

The method of solution can easily be formulated as an algorithm:

1) Add the first column with carry.
2) Add the following column, with carry if necessary (and create a carry if required).
3) Repeat 2 until all columns have been processed.

This algorithm does not take into account the case when a carry occurs in the last place. This can be accomplished as follows:

4) If a carry occurs in the last column, extend the result by one place and write the carry in this place.

If the extension by one place is not possible (as is often the case), an error can also be generated to indicate overflow. Several numbers can be added by successive execution of the algorithm.

As this point we should ask ourselves if the method of solution is mathematically valid, and if it always leads to the correct result. With this simple example, we would hardly doubt our solution. But it is possible to prove that our column addition is valid:

```
235 = 2*10² + 3*10¹ + 5*10⁰
582 = 5*102 + 8*101 + 2*100

235 + 582 ................  =    (2*10² + 3*10¹ + 5*10⁰)
                                +(5*10² + 8*10¹ + 2*10⁰) =
                                 (2+5)*10² + (3+8)*10¹ + (5+2)*10⁰=
                                 7*10² + 11*10¹ + 7*10⁰=
                                 7*10² + 1*10² + 1*10¹ + 7*10⁰=
                                 8*10² + 1*10¹ + 7*10⁰=
                                 817
```

In this explanation we have used the commutative and associative properties, among others. But we have proven the procedure only for this example. The proof for other examples can be formulated similarly.

In practice, you won't prove each algorithm mathematically before using it. Many perfectly correct algorithms cannot be so proven because they are too complex or complicated. In other words, no one has found (or looked for...) a proof for these algorithms, at least as of yet. In many instances it is reasonable to check the algorithm for mathematical correctness. Errors (such as exception cases) can often be found this way.

Multiplication can be performed in a manner similar to addition. The general procedure is well known:

```
    243 * 103
    -----------
          729
            0
+     243
    -----------
    25029
```

In this algorithm, column-type multiplications are performed first. The results of these multiplications are added, being valued according to the place at which a factor stands.

Note the partial multiplications by "1" and "0". For a partial multiplication by "0", only a zero is written down below, and by a "1", simply the original factor "243".

With this short introduction we wanted simply to look at the decimal system in order to be able to recognize analogies between computation procedures in the various number systems.

How is data represented in the computer?

There are many ways to represent data or numbers in computers. You could assign a voltage to each number proportional to its value—such as 1.23 Volts for the number 1.23. This principle is used in analog computers. The disadvantage of this methods is obvious—all computer components and memory units must work very precisely. With a required calculation accuracy of three places, the deviation must be under one-thousandth. With a range of 4 places, voltages between 0.01 and 10 must be recognized and processed precisely. In addition, the number range is limited. Other disadvantages of analog computers are that they are harder to program, and in practice can only process numerical values.

For representing numbers in a computer we must select a well-suited number system with place notation. You might naturally choose the decimal system. Immediately a question is raised: how is a digit represented? Again, the problem is differentiating between the ten individual digits.

We are able to prove mathematically the number of possibilities per digit a number system should have to be most effective. Thankfully this has been done for us already; the number arrived at was 2.7. Rounded off we get 3. Consequently, we have the digits 0,1, and 2 available. But limiting the number of possibilities per digit to two is technically simpler and less prone to error. As a result, the binary system was chosen for computers.

In the binary system, each place has only two possible conditions—namely "0" and "1". These two conditions can also be represented easily. For example:

"0"	"1"
Voltage absent	Voltage present
No current flowing	Current flowing
Relay not making contact	Relay making contact
Switch off	Switch on
Lamp off	Lamp on

The abbreviated term "bit" was derived from the phrase "binary digit." A bit is therefore a two-value digit; it can be only "0" or "1".

As in the decimal system, larger numbers can be represented in place notation. It is simple to write several bits in succession. The base in the binary system is naturally two, and not ten as in the decimal system.

The binary number "0101" is therefore an abbreviation of:

$$0*2^3 + 1*2^2 + 0*2^1 + 1*2^0$$

The principle is exactly the same as for the decimal system. Since the base is two, it has to be "2^x", and not "10^x" as in the decimal system. The binary number "0101" can be converted to the decimal system directly:

$$0*2^3 + 1*2^2 + 0*2^1 + 1*2^0 = 5$$

Naturally, larger binary numbers can also be converted to decimal numbers. As an example we take "01101110":

$$
\begin{array}{rcl}
0 * 2^7 & = & 0 * 128 = 0 \\
+1 * 2^6 & = & 1 * 64 = 64 \\
+1 * 2^5 & = & 1 * 32 = 32 \\
+0 * 2^4 & = & 0 * 16 = 0 \\
+1 * 2^3 & = & 1 * 8 = 8 \\
+1 * 2^2 & = & 1 * 4 = 4 \\
+1 * 2^1 & = & 1 * 2 = 2 \\
+0 * 2^0 & = & 0 * 1 = 0 \\
\hline
& & 110
\end{array}
$$

To avoid confusion concerning the base of a number , we will indicate a binary number by placing a "%" in front of it (such as %01101110 = 110). Decimal numbers receive no additional indication.

Naturally, you can convert a decimal number to a binary number as well. We will use 110 as an example again. The following method can be used:

$$
\begin{array}{lll}
110 / 2 = 55 & \quad & \text{remainder: } 0 \\
55 / 2 = 27 & & \text{remainder: } 1 \\
27 / 2 = 13 & & \text{remainder: } 1 \\
13 / 2 = 6 & & \text{remainder: } 1 \\
6 / 2 = 3 & & \text{remainder: } 0 \\
3 / 2 = 1 & & \text{remainder: } 1 \\
1 / 2 = 1 & & \text{remainder: } 1
\end{array}
$$

The remainder column yields the binary number, read from bottom to top, in our example %1101110. Clearly %1101110 = %01101110. This also gives us the proof for our first conversion.

You can compute with binary numbers using the same procedures used for decimal numbers. Just remember that only two digits are available. A carry occurs "beyond" 1 already, and not first at "9" as in the decimal system.

An addition of two binary numbers looks like this:

```
        0110
   +    1011
   ------------
       10001              ( 6 + 11 = 17 )
```

At this point it would be a good idea to try out some examples of this method. Also, practice the conversions to and from the decimal system.

Multiplication of binary numbers is also performed in the same way as decimal numbers. Since only the digits "0" and "1" occur in the binary system, only the zero and the first factor are added. We made a corresponding observation in the multiplication of decimal numbers. As an example we will calculate %0110 * %1011:

```
   0110     *      1011
            ---------------
                0110
                0110
                0000
            +   0110
            ----------
                1000010      ( 6 * 11 = 66 )
```

Subtraction can be performed as usual, but taking the different base into account. Another way to perform subtraction is by adding a negative number; to do this, you must first consider how a negative number is represented in binary. We make the following consideration:

If we add %1 to the number %1111, *without* taking the carry into account, we get %0000. The reverse would be to subtract one from %0000. Then we clearly get %1111 back. So %1111 corresponds to "-1". In order to make a clear designation, the highest order bit is defined as the sign bit. If it is a "1", the number is negative; if a "0", it is positive.

When computing with negative binary numbers it is important to ensure that both numbers have the same number of digits (bits).

The negative numbers can be easily recognized:

```
%1100 %1101 %1110 %1111 %0000 %0001 %0010 %0011
 -4    -3    -2    -1     0     1     2     3
```

You may have figured out that for a given number of bits, there is always one more negative number than positive. With four bits, we can get the numbers -8...7, and with eight bits the numbers -128...127.

A negative binary number easily can be converted from a negative decimal number. First the corresponding positive decimal number is converted to binary. Then all the bits of the binary number are reversed—a "1" bit becomes a "0" and vice versa. The procedure is called generating the "one's complement." To this one's complement you then add one, this result in the negative binary number and is called the two's complement.

Example:

```
-5  :              5 =   %0101
    One's complement of     %0101      =      %1010
                                       +      %0001
                                       =      %1011
Result:                      -5        =      %1011
```

```
   5 - 4 :                      3 - 6 :

(5)    %0101              (3)    %0011
(-4) + %1100             (-6) + %1010
-----------              -------------

(1)    %0001             (-3)   %1101
```

If the carry is not taken into account in the addition (example "5 - 4"), we get the correct result. With this type of calculation, you must limit the number range. Since in microcomputers the number range is always limited, this is no difficulty in practice.

Without a complete proof, we have shown here that the representation really works—we can add and subtract (adding the negative numbers).

In order to convert a 4-bit binary number to an 8-bit binary number, we have to take into account the value of the highest-order bit (the sign bit) of the 4-bit number. If this bit is zero, the top four bits of the 8-bit binary number are filled with %0000, and otherwise with "1111". For example:

4-bit binary number	8-bit binary number
%0110	%00000110
%1111	%11111111
%1001	%11111001
%0100	%00000100

When converting 8-bit binary numbers to 4-bit binary numbers, the top (left-most) four bits are simply stripped off. However, a check must first be made to see if the number will fit into four bits.

Naturally, this principle applies to more than just 4 and 8-bit binary numbers. It can be applied to all other combinations as well.

It's obvious that representing numbers in binary makes them hard for mere humans to read. It is much easier for us to work with a number like 110 than with its binary equivalent, %01101110. To form a direct bridge between the numbers with which computers work, and numbers that humans prefer (numbers with fewer places required), it makes sense to combine several binary places together. This way the computer can continue to work in binary internally, while we use numbers with fewer places externally.

Unfortunately, combining places does not work with the decimal system. This is because ten is not an integer power of two. All binary possibilities of the combined binary places must have a correspondence with the new digits. If we take three bits at a time, the digits 0...7 can be expressed. Since the digits 8 and 9 are not required, we cannot use the usual decimal notation. On the other hand, if we group four binary digits together, the bit combinations %0000...%1001 can be expressed by the digits 0...9. The remaining bit combinations have correspondence in the decimal system.

It becomes clear that the number systems familiar to us will not work. For the base of the number system we are looking for, we must use a number that is a power of two. In theory and in practice, we have only two options: the numbers 8 and 16.

If we want to use 8, we must group exactly three bits, since three bits give us 2^3=8 combinations. The number system resulting from this grouping is called the octal system. It found widespread use in older mainframe computers. The reason for this is that the digits in the octal system are only a subset of the digits in the decimal system. You need not introduce any "new" digits, so every printer that can output decimal digits (such as the printing mechanism of calculators) can also output octal digits. The following table contrasts binary, octal, and decimal numbers:

Decimal	Binary	Octal
0	000	0
1	001	1
2	010	2
3	011	3
4	100	4
5	101	5
6	110	6
7	111	7
8	1000	10
9	1001	11
10	1010	12
11	1011	13
12	1100	14
13	1101	15
14	1110	16
15	1111	17
16	10000	20

Computations can be performed in the octal system as they would be in any other of our number systems. If you are interested, try a few problems. You can check your work by converting to the corresponding binary representation and then to the decimal system, and back again.

The main disadvantage of the octal system is that one decimal place cannot be stored in the field for one octal digit. In other words, numbers 8 and 9 cannot be represented "one for one." To represent the digits "8" and "9" we need a second octal digit.

This disadvantage is eliminated when we group four bits together. Since four bits give 2^4=16 bit combinations, the base of the resulting system is 16. This number system is called the hexadecimal system.

In order to represent the sixteen combinations, six new characters are required in addition to the ten "normal" digits. For the sake of simplicity, the letters A through F are used. The table below shows the conversion between the various number systems:

Decimal	Binary	Octal	Hexadecimal
0	0000	0	0
1	0001	1	1
2	0010	2	2
3	0011	3	3
4	0100	4	4
5	0101	5	5
6	0110	6	6
7	0111	7	7
8	1000	10	8
9	1001	11	9
10	1010	12	A
11	1011	13	B
12	1100	14	C
13	1101	15	D
14	1110	16	E
15	1111	17	F
16	10000	20	10
23	10111	27	17
24	11000	30	18
32	100000	40	20

The conversion from hexadecimal to decimal follows the same principle as that from binary to decimal. Since it is used so often, here's an example.

The hexadecimal number "C57A" is just an abbreviated notation for:

$$C*16^3 + 5*16^2 + 7*16^1 + A*16^0$$

or, written another way:

$$12*16^3 + 5*16^2 + 7*16^1 + 10*16^0 = 50554$$

There are two possibilities for the conversion back to hexadecimal. The simplest is to convert the decimal number to its binary equivalent and then convert the binary number to hexadecimal. However, this procedure requires a large number of computational steps.

The other procedure is more difficult, but gets the result faster:

> The number to be converted is divided by the largest power of sixteen that is smaller than the number itself. The number after the decimal point is then multiplied by sixteen.

As an example, let's take the number 50554. The largest power of 16 smaller than 50554 is 16^3=4096; 16^4 is already 65536.

```
50554 / 4096   =12.34228516 ==:12 (decimal) = C (hex)
0.3442285 *16  =5.476562499 ==: 5 (decimal) = 5 (hex)
0.47656 * 16   =7.624999987 ==: 7 (decimal) = 7 (hex)
0.625 * 16     =10           ==:10 (decimal) = A (hex)
```

At this point we stop because we divided by the third power of 16. Our result is (as expected) "C57A". It should be noted that calculation does not always "come out even." In this case we were just "lucky" with the rounding-off. In any event, you should practice this process if you have no other way of converting hex numbers.

We denote hexadecimal numbers by placing a $ in front of them. We would write the hexadecimal number "C57A" as $C57A.

Calculations can be performed with hexadecimal numbers as with decimal numbers. You need only note that a carry does not occur until "F", instead of "9".

Example of "hex addition":

```
      C5D9
  +   13EA
  -------
      D9C3
```

At first glance this looks complicated, but it can be easily explained:

```
$9+$A =9+10 =19 =16+3 =(carry $1) + $3
(carry $1)+$D+$E =1+13+14 =28 =16+12 =(carry $1)+$C
(carry $1)+$5+$3 =1+5+3 =9 =$9
$C+$1 =12+1 =13 =$D
```

You will be seeing such calculations more often, since computers work fundamentally with bits, and these are almost always gathered into hex numbers. The multiplication of hex numbers is usually performed as multiplication of the binary representation of the factors.

Negative binary numbers in two's complement can also be written as hex numbers, and processed as such.

Example:

$$-95 = \$A1 = \%1010001$$

The same rules applying to computation with negative binary numbers in two's complement also apply to computation with negative hex numbers in two's complement. In the final analysis, hexadecimal representation is only an abbreviated notation for binary representation.

At this point we could write more about working with hex numbers, but it would be difficult to remember everything if we explained it now. In particular, we will explain how calculations are performed with the MC68000 microprocessor in a later chapter.

Representation of decimal fractions

So far we haven't said anything about how decimal fractions are represented in a computer. We will just give some examples, since we do not have enough space to explain in detail here. But these decimal fractions are important, especially so as we learn machine language programming.

A widely-used form of representation of decimal fractions is what's known as the normalized exponential representation. In the number 0.0000234, four places (the four zeros after the decimal) are required just to indicate where the decimal goes. This number can also be written as

$0.234*10^{-5}$. The number -100 can be written as $-0.1*10^3$, 41.23 as $0.4123*10^2$. The 0.4123 (in the last example) is usually called the mantissa, and the 2 is called the exponent.

This method of representation can also be carried over to binary numbers. You call also write the binary number 1010.011 as $0.1010011*2^4$.

Binary numbers in exponential notation can be represented in the computer in various formats. One commonly used format is 32 bits for representation:

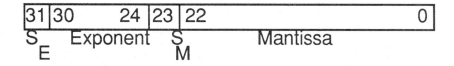

S_E : sign of the exponent S_M : sign of the mantissa

In this example, both the exponent and the mantissa are represented in two's complement. The exponent can therefore accept the values -128..127. There are 24 bits available for the mantissa. Since the first bit indicates the sign, 23 bits remain for the amount.

This is obviously just one example of representation in the normalized exponential form. The number of bits used can be varied, of course.

Conversion errors always arise when converting from decimal to binary or hexadecimal and back again. Binary representations are not well-suited for applications requiring absolute accuracy (such as corporate business applications, and shuttle launches). To perform such calculations, there is another form of representation.

BCD representation

BCD is an acronym for Binary-Coded Decimal. In BCD, each four bits represent a decimal digit. It must be note that the computation rules for binary numbers *cannot* be applied to BCD numbers. BCD numbers have the same form as binary numbers, but have other properties.

The number 735 would be represented as follows:

```
735 = 0111 0011 0101   (BCD)
```

Note that a number like 1101 0111 0101 is not a BCD number, because 1101 doesn't represent a decimal digit (it represents 13 or D).

Additional "tricks" are often used to represent BCD numbers efficiently. For example, the first BCD digit can indicate how many places the number has. The second digit can determine whether the number is positive or negative (%0000 = +, %0001 = -):

```
0011    0001    0111    0011    0101
  3       -       7       3       5
```

This grouping would represent -735 according to this BCD convention (3 places, negative, quantity=735).

Decimal fractions can be similarly represented. A BCD digit that indicates the position of the decimal point (counting from the right) can be inserted between the first two groups of four:

0011	0010	0001	0111	0011	0101
3	2	–	7	3	5

This grouping would indicate -7.35 (3 places, decimal at the second position from the right, negative, quantity=735).

There are many similar representations, of course, but we only want to present the principle here.

Nibbles, bytes, etc.

Often several bits are used together. Some names for various "groupings" of bits have come into common use. We will not make an attempt to explain their origin, but merely present them:

1 **nibble**	corresponds to	4 bits
1 **byte**	corresponds to	8 bits
1 **word**	corresponds to	16 bits
1 **long word**	corresponds to	32 bits

Accordingly, a byte contains two nibbles, a word contains four nibbles, a long word contains four bytes, and so on. A nibble can be written as one hexadecimal digit. The larger groupings are usually written as multiple hexadecimal digits. Naturally, they can all be written as binary, but already at the byte level this becomes difficult to read. The octal system is not well-suited for specifying values, since neither 4 nor 8, 16, or 32 is divisible by 3, and the octal digits are not used efficiently.

Representing letters

As we know, the computer always stores data in binary. In order to be able to process letter characters (a, b, c, d...) in the computer, we must define a code that assigns a unique bit combination to each character.

Such a code has been in use for a long time: the telex code. The telex code uses 5 bits, giving a total of 32 bit combinations. Although the telex uses only lower case letters, the number of combinations is not enough. In addition to the 26 letters, 10 digits are required. A trick is used to represent the digits and punctuation characters. Two code levels are used in parallel. One contains all of the letters, while the other contains the special characters (like ":", "=", etc.). Switching between the letters and the special characters is done with two non-printing control characters. Two control characters, the control character for carriage return & line feed, and the one for a space, exist in both code levels with the same bit combinations.

If, for example, you send the bit combination %01100, an "i" is printed if the letter code level is active. The digit and special character code level is enabled by the control character %11011. Now the code %01100 causes the character "8" to be printed. The code %00100 represents the space character, regardless of the active code level.

Because of this switching of the code levels, the telex code is inconvenient to use. Another disadvantage is that the upper case letters are not present. But for a long time, many computer hobbyists used telex machines for printers. In 1982 a used telex machine could be purchased for less than $100, while a computer printer would cost at least $500. But since printer prices have fallen so dramatically, there is little interest in trying to cope with the disadvantages (not to mention noise and slow speed) of a telex machine.

Another code that allows the representation of all of the usual characters is the EBCDIC code from IBM. This would be of interest only to those who want to work with IBM mainframes.

The most widely-used code is the ASCII code. ASCII (pronounced as-key) is an abbreviation for American Standard Code for Information Interchange.

Twenty-six upper-case and and 26 lower-case letters must be represented in the English language. In addition, 10 digits and about 20 special characters are required. This results in a total number of 82 representable characters. In order to represent this many characters as bit combinations, but without having to use code levels like the telex, 7 bits are required. The ASCII code is in fact a 7-bit code. The remaining combinations are used as control characters for line feed, carriage return, etc. In addition, there are several control codes that control the data traffic to and from peripheral devices.

Since seven is an "uneven" number, ASCII characters are usually represented with eight bits. Then an ASCII character is exactly as wide as a byte. This has decisive advantages when storing data. The eighth bit is often used for error checking, to enable various character sets or type sizes, etc.

On the next page is a table of the ASCII code. The combinations in the first section of the first column (0-31) represent the control characters. Many of these are used only rarely in practice. The following are the most important for learning machine language:

BEL   Bell
BS   Back space
LF   Line feed
FF   Form feed
CR   Carriage return

The standard ASCII character set contains no foreign language characters. Some of the unused bit combinations in the 7-bit code are frequently used for these missing characters.

The ASCII CODE

DEC	HEX	ASCII	CTRL	DEC	HEX	ASCII	DEC	HEX	ASCII
0	00	NUL	@	43	2B	+	85	55	U
1	01	SOH	A	44	2C	,	86	56	V
2	02	STX	B	45	2D	-	87	57	W
3	03	ETX	C	46	2E	.	88	58	X
4	04	EOT	D	47	2F	/	89	59	Y
5	05	ENQ	E	48	30	0	90	5A	Z
6	06	ACK	F	49	31	1	91	5B	[
7	07	BEL	G	50	32	2	92	5C	\
8	08	BS	H	51	33	3	93	5D	]
9	09	HF	I	52	34	4	94	5E	^
10	0A	LF	J	53	35	5	95	5F	_
11	0B	VT	K	54	36	6	96	60	'
12	0C	FF	L	55	37	7	97	61	a
13	0D	CR	M	56	38	8	98	62	b
14	0E	SO	N	57	39	9	99	63	c
15	0F	SI	O	58	3A	:	100	64	d
16	10	DLE	P	59	3B	;	101	65	e
17	11	DC1	Q	60	3C	<	102	66	f
18	12	DC2	R	61	3D	=	103	67	g
19	13	DC3	S	62	3E	>	104	68	h
20	14	DC4	T	63	3F	?	105	69	i
21	15	NAK	U	64	40	@	106	6A	j
22	16	SYN	V	65	41	A	107	6B	k
23	17	ETB	W	66	42	B	108	6C	l
24	18	CAN	X	67	43	C	109	6D	m
25	19	EM	Y	68	44	D	110	6E	n
26	1A	SUB	Z	69	45	E	111	6F	o
27	1B	ESC	[	70	46	F	112	70	p
28	1C	FS	\	71	47	G	113	71	q
29	1D	GS	]	72	48	H	114	72	r
30	1E	RS	^	73	49	I	115	73	s
31	1F	US	_	74	4A	J	116	74	t
32	20	Space		75	4B	K	117	75	u
33	21	!		76	4C	L	118	76	v
34	22	"		77	4D	M	119	77	w
35	23	#		78	4E	N	120	78	x
36	24	$		79	4F	O	121	79	y
37	25	%		80	50	P	122	7A	z
38	26	&		81	51	Q	123	7B	{
39	27	'		82	52	R	124	7C	|
40	28	(		83	53	S	125	7D	}
41	29	)		84	54	T	126	7E	~
42	2A	*					127	7F	DEL

Logical operations and bit manipulation

In addition to the more familiar arithmetic operations (addition, multiplication, etc.) there are also some logical operations. Logical operations, in contrast to arithmetic operations, affect only the individual bits. Furthermore, a logical operation can be either unary or binary—that is, it may have one or two operands. There are four particularly important logical operations, as shown below:

NOT			AND		
A	NOT A		A	B	A AND B
0	1		0	0	0
1	0		0	1	0
			1	0	0
			1	1	1

OR			EXOR		
A	B	A OR B	A	B	A EXOR B
0	0	0	0	0	0
0	1	1	0	1	1
1	0	1	1	0	1
1	1	1	1	1	0

For "0" we say "false," and "true" for "1". Then we see that the logical operators shown here correspond to the usual logical operators in mathematics. An example of logical operators:

An "0" in A signals that the weather is bad;
a "1" that the weather is good.

A "1" in B signals that it's the weekend;
a "0" that it is not the weekend.

If you want to go swimming on the weekend when the weather is good, you could say that (A **AND** B) must be "1". The expression (A **OR** B) would mean that you would go swimming if only one of the criteria were fulfilled. The expression (A **EXOR** B) means that exactly one of the criteria may be fulfilled.

Naturally, these logical operators can be combined with each other and thereby form new logical operators. These can then combine three or more bits with each other.

Back to our example. We do not go swimming when "**NOT** (A and B)" is "1". The expression "((**NOT** (A)) or (**NOT** (B)))" is equivalent to "**NOT** (A and B)". This can be proven mathematically.

Logical operators can be used on bytes, words, or more generally on multiple bits, or bit fields. The operation is simply performed bit by bit with the corresponding bits of the operands.

29

We have already seen one example. We have formed the one's complement of a binary number. We simply "reversed" the individual bits. This corresponds to the bitwise execution of the **NOT** function.

Another example:

$$\textbf{NOT}\ (0010)\quad =\ 1101$$

The following are examples of the other logical operations:

```
   (0010)         (0010)            (0010)
OR(1011)      AND(1011)      EXOR(1011)
--------      ----------      ----------
= 1011         = 0010            = 1001
```

These operations are often used to make intentional, conditional changes of bits. The operators are often written differently. We will explain the notation at the appropriate point later.

Bit shift operations

In addition to the logical operations, there are operations that shift the individual bits of a binary number. The MC68000 in your Atari ST has a number of commands to do this. We will simply present some examples here. We'll take the binary number %00101100.

Shifted one position to the right, it reads %00010110 (provided the free place is filled with a zero). If we take into account the value of the number, we see that it has been reduced by half. As a rule, shifting to the right corresponds to a division of the binary number by two.

Shifting one position to the left results in the original number becoming %01011000. Now the value has doubled. As a rule, shifting to the left corresponds to a multiplication of the binary number by two.

In addition to these bit-shifting operations, there are operations that rotate bits. For example, %10011000 rotated one position to the left becomes %00110001.

Program development

When you're starting to write a program, you first must know exactly what you are trying to solve. Consequently, you must determine the end result. To do this, you must first clarify what data should be printed out. It seems quite logical, but first, what do we mean by "data"? One definition:

Data: *any representation of characters, symbols, and letters that are to be processed in some manner.*

In addition to this you should note that data *also* may represent decisions, logical conditions, etc.

After determining the problem and specifying the end result (data printout), you should determine clearly the source of the data to be processed. Next, you usually make an exact data flow plan. This data flow plan can take almost any form, depending on the preferences of the programmer. Whatever its form, the data flow plan must clearly determine the course of the processing, the input/output, the storage, etc. Now the exact algorithm should be developed. Under certain circumstances existing algorithms that satisfactorily solve the problem can be found. Why re-invent the wheel, after all?

When all of the above is done, a flow chart or structogram (sometimes both) is created. (More information on flow charts and structograms can be found in chapter 5). Here the breakdown and routing of the data flow is refined, and sometimes the algorithm has to be reformulated.

Not until this is done should the program be formulated in the selected programming language. Often parts of the program are written in a high-level language (BASIC, Pascal, C etc.), while other sections are written in machine language (assembly language). Time-critical portions are often written in machine language because it is usually much faster than high-level languages.

Not until the program is completely written should it be tried on the computer. Programming by trial and error is not particularly sensible (no matter how often it's done by the general population). It is important to test the program from as many different angles and viewpoints as possible. Errors often occur under unexpected conditions.

After the actual program is finished, the program documentation is prepared. This should make it possible for the programmer, and others, to change the program later. Without good documentation, sometimes even *you* won't be able to understand your own programs after a year or two.

Also important is the creation of a user's guide. The user's guide is important in determining the actual utility that the program has for others. Naturally, the target audience must taken into account. A program intended for a programmer's use must be described differently than a program to be used by a secretary with no knowledge of computers.

Even after the program is "finished," your work on it is not done. Errors discovered by users must be corrected; changes in other circumstances must be taken into account (for instance, revised tax laws as they affect your income tax program). And the actual use of the program almost always shows that it lacks something. These post-programming situations come under the heading Program Maintenance.

In summary, the phases of program development are as follows:

1) Exact specification of the problem
2) Creation of a data-flow plan
3) Writing a flowchart or structogram
4) Writing the program in a programming language
5) Entering program, testing it, correcting errors
6) Program documentation
7) User's guide
8) Program maintenance

In practice, these phases/steps obviously can become blurred. But in principle, a good programmer will try to work according to this plan. A good programmer doesn't sit down at the computer and not get up again until the program is done; he/she follows the above plan intelligently. Often individual processes are carried out in your head (especially with small programs). This procedure divides large programs up into smaller programs, making it possible for several people to work on the project independently, without hindering each other. Naturally, the tasks must be carefully defined beforehand to make this process work.

Probably the biggest problem is that only 10% of all programmers are actually able to work with an exact concept and plan—but the other 90% believe they belong to this 10%.

Chapter Two

Hardware Fundamentals

- •Introduction
- •Memory
- •Central processing unit
- •Input/output

Introduction

A computer consists of three basic components:

Memory
Central processing unit
Input/output devices

However, these three components are not three neatly-packaged electronic chips; there are considerably more than three components in the Atari ST. Several integrated cicuits are required to perform each of the functions listed above.

Memory

There are basically two types of memory:

1) Read/write memory (RAM)
            and
2) Read-only memory (ROM)

The read/write memory is also called RAM, which stands for Random Access Memory. The primary difference between RAM and ROM is that you can write to RAM memory, while the content of ROM is fixed and unchangeable.

You can picture RAM as a dresser with several drawers. Let's assume that our dresser has six drawers, organized as two rows of three drawers. We then can picture the six drawers in two ways:

1)

0	1	2
3	4	5

This gives us drawers 0...5 that we can clearly distinguish between. (Computer scientists almost always start counting at zero, which has its advantages when working with computers and their programs). There is also another way to picture these drawers:

2)

	0	1	2
0	0	1	2
1	0	1	2

Here we get the names   (0,0), (0,1), (0,2)
                            (1,0), (1,1), (1,2)

Again, all of the drawers can be identified individually, with no ambiguity. We want to remember these two methods of numbering for the future. The first is called linear ordering; the second we will refer to as matrix ordering.

Note that from a hardware perspective, memory is seen as a matrix of a certain size; but from a software point of view, the memory locations are thought of and addressed linearly. (To confuse things, matrices are also *programmed* in a linear fashion—but we won't get into this).

In our case we have six distinct drawers we want to put to use. Let's open drawer zero and see what is inside:

Nothing

Why nothing? Because we haven't put anything into it! But then again, is nothing really *Nothing*? This question is quite philosophical. We'll stray a bit from this topic in order to clarify three very important computer science terms. These terms will help us answer the above question—at least for our purposes!

The computer scientist distinguishes between three characteristics of information:

> 1) the syntactic,
> 2) the semantic, and
> 3) the pragmatic aspects of information.

By first term, *syntactic*, we mean the primary ordered structure of information. Take any word, say "man." If we mean "man" but instead write "one," no one would understand us. So we keep to the rules of English (syntax rules) and write "man."

A traffic light provides another example. The syntax of a traffic light is:

red

yellow

green

If two of the colors were to appear simultaneously, no one would understand the traffic light. This would be syntactically false.

By *semantic* we mean the content of the information, or the intended meaning of the information. Said another way, the semantic meaning is the effect the message has when stated. For example, the semantic aspect of the red light is "STOP." This is the intended message of a red light.

The third way to view a piece of information is *pragmatically*. It indicates the utility of the information to the end user; in other words, how *you* might use the information. For example, if you see a yellow light, you might think "No problem, I can still make it"; another mental reaction you might have is "Whoa! better put on the brakes."

With these definitions we can answer the philosophically unanswerable question, "We see nothing in the drawer just opened." At least for our pragmatic purposes, the answer is: the drawer holds

Nothing that we can use

According to our three points:

1) The syntax of the information is valid; something is certainly in the drawer, even if it is just a vacuum.

2) The semantic meaning is also clear: we put nothing in, so we can't get anything out.

3) Viewed pragmatically, the drawer, for us, is empty—even though something (namely *Nothing*) is in it! We can put anything we want into it. If we chose the put something in the drawer, and neither we nor anyone else takes it out again, we will always find it there when we open the drawer.

Now we'll technically formulate the procedure described above. We will call the numbers we gave to the drawers **addresses**.

And exactly eight bits will fit into each drawer!

Now we open a drawer, such as number 3. The process of opening a drawer we will call **addressing**.

Looking into it we will call	**reading**
Putting something in we call	**writing**
The drawer itself is called	**memory location**

In time we'll learn to use all of these terms properly.

So, let's **address** the **memory location 3** and **read** it. What is in it? Nothing, of course; we haven't written anything into it.

As we learned in the previous chapter, only zeros and ones can be in a memory location, since we have only two digits. Moreover, we have just said that nothing need not be nothing (absolutely or philosophically). It may be that the number %01101100 ($6C) is there. Why?

Technically, this random number being in the drawer can be explained. Due to the unevenness of the conductive traces within a computer's electronic components, the memory contains random, arbitrary bit combinations after power-up. These bit combinations can be any of the 256 combinations of eight zeros and ones, namely %00000000 to %11111111.

Let's assume that we have a computer that, after being turned on, contains the hex number $6C in memory location 3.

We can **read** this value at any time, since it is in the drawer. However, the pragmatic portion of this information is negligible; we have no use for this purely random information.

So we want to **write** some real data into it. We select "$D7". We address our memory location number 3 and write the number $D7 to it.

What happens? The random number $6C leaves memory location 3 and the $D7 is **stored**. When we later access memory location 3, we will always read the number $D7 until we write a new number into the memory location or turn the computer off. Should we write a new number into the memory location, the $D7 obviously will be **overwritten** by the new number. If we turn the computer off, we'll again get random data when the computer is turned back on.

Isn't there any way to retrieve stored information in RAM and protect it from being overwritten after we turn the computer off?

For us, the answer is no—unless we modify with the circuitry of the computer. RAM is read/write memory. If we want to have memory that gives us useful information but cannot be overwritten, we must use read-only memory. If we absolutely, positively have to protect the information in RAM when the computer is turned off, the RAMs must be supplied with current after all of the components have been turned off. For this purpose, there are RAMs that use very little current and may be backed up by a battery circuit. The Atari ST, however, uses "normal" RAMs.

Read-Only Memory

Read-only memory is called ROM. There are many types of ROM, and these are differentiated by the letters preceding ROM: EPROM, EEROM, EAROM, PROM, IPROM.

But all these types of ROMs have one thing in common. Without outside tampering, the computer cannot change the information contained in ROM. In some of the components, the information is embedded in them when the chip is made so that it can never be altered (except, of course, by destroying the component itself).

Central processing unit

The central processing unit manages the whole computer. It addresses the available memory, handles data in the memory, and manages or directs the peripherals. It is the heart of every computer; if defective, nothing in the computer will work properly.

Generally, the CPU consists of some internal memory locations called registers; in contrast to the usual memory, registers have the advantage that they can be addressed almost instantly by the central processing unit. The CPU also has circuits for controlling the memory and I/O lines, the complex logic for computation, as well as internal temporary storage that cannot be directly addressed.

The CPU supplies address signals for controlling the other components, data lines for transferring data (reading or writing), and control signals indicating the status of the CPU (such as a read/write line, which indicates whether data is being sent or being read).

The CPU used in the Atari ST is the MC68000. This chip has 24 address lines; therefore, 2^{24} (1, 677, 216) different bytes can theoretically be addressed in memory. Naturally, the actual memory of the ST is not this large—extensive areas of addressing range are unused.

The 68000 is a 16-bit microprocessor. This means that the data bus (the lines over which data flow to and from the microprocessor) is 16 bits wide. Therefore, the memory is also 16 bits wide. Two bytes (one word) are always accessed together in the memory. Each of these bytes has its own address because the 68000 is a byte-oriented machine. But since the data bus can transport both bytes at once, it is possible to write or read the entire memory word in one access. There is one condition for this: a word access can be made to even-numbered addresses only.

Input/Output

A computer has input/output components that allow it to communicate with the "outside world." The keyboard is an example of an input components; the mouse is also an input device. On the Atari ST, output goes to the screen or to a printer. Sounds it creates and plays on the speakers are outputs, also.

The disk drives are connected to the Atari ST via a special component called a floppy controller, also an input/output device. The disk drives are not counted as normal memory because the data cannot be simply addressed as it is in the normal RAM/ROM memory.

The data can be transferred from a peripheral to memory in two ways:

1) The processor itself reads the data from the   peripheral device or outputs the address itself. It usually accesses a register in the peripheral. The access resembles that of a normal memory location. The transmission can be initiated in one of two ways: a) the microprocessor continually checks to see if data is available or required (this is called "polling"); or b) while in the middle of executing some program, it is interrupted by a hardware signal from the peripheral that tells it when data is available or required. The first method is like having someone constantly waiting by the telephone. A drawback of this technique is that time is required to see if someone is on the phone. With the second technique, no time is wasted if the telephone isn't ringing.

2) The processor initializes the data transfer in a DMA controller (DMA: Direct Memory Access). The processor determines what data from which memory range is to be transferred to a new memory location. The actual transfer from memory to peripheral device (and vice versa) is performed by the DMA controller . On a signal from the peripheral device, the DMA controller takes over control of the system bus and performs the data transfer itself. The main processor is relieved of this burden, and as a result the whole system is more efficient. Not until the entire transmission is complete is the main processor notified by the DMA controller that the bus is free for other purposes. The main processor can also check to see if the transfer is done. This DMA transfer is usually made much faster than other transfer types.

The following analogy can be made to a DMA transfer:

You ask your friend to telephone a local auto dealer and get the prices of all late-model Porsches on the lot. You tell him that when he has all of the information he should put it in your mailbox, and ring the doorbell. In the meantime, you'll be having a candlelight dinner with an intimate acquaintance. Your hear the doorbell ring after the main course, retrieve the Porsche prices, and impress your guest during dessert...

Chapter Three

The 68000 Microprocessor

- Introduction
- Register structure and data organization
- Operating states
- Addressing modes
- Overview of the instruction set

Introduction

This chapter is intended to give a brief overview of the structure of the Atari ST's MC68000 microprocessor. First we'll explain a few terms used throughout the remainder of the book. An exact description of all of the 68000's instructions is beyond the scope of this book; only the most useful of the instructions are explained. Exceptions will be explained in principle only, for their exact description does not belong in a book intended to teach machine language.

We advise you to get a book on the 68000 processor and its instructions. Even if you already know machine language programming, you will still need a 68000 reference work; in it you will also find the instructions not explained here. Now let's proceed wth the terminology.

The 68000 has two different addressing modes. These are called the **supervisor** and the **user** modes. Of these two, only the supervisor mode allows use of all instructions. The supervisor mode makes it possible to build "exit-proof" multi-user systems.

For example, the operating system can be run in the supervisor mode at the same time user programs run in the user mode. In the Atari ST, the memory and peripheral area at the bottom of the address range can be accessed only when the processor is in the supervisor mode. In the user mode, the program is halted and an error-handling routine is called. Other systems have components called MMUs (Memory Management Units) that monitor which addresses are accessed. If an attempt is made to access "forbidden" area, the MMU interrupts the program.

Register structure and data organization

The 68000 has eight data registers available to the user. Each of these data registers has a width of 32 bits. For this reason, the 68000 is often referred to as a 32-bit processor . But since its data bus is only 16 bits wide, it is considered a 16-bit processor. The data registers are named **D0** to **D7**.

In addition to the data registers, there are seven address registers and a program counter. Again, these registers are 32 bits wide. This results in an address range of 4 gigabytes. But because the 68000's address bus is only 24 bits wide, only 16 megabytes are available. The address registers are named A0...A6. The program counter is referred to as **PC**.

Because there is a large number registers, it is possible to store many variables in the registers and limit the number of memory accesses within a program. Since the registers are 32 bits wide, they can also contain an entire memory address.

Furthermore, there are two stack pointers, one for the user mode and one for the supervisor mode. Exactly one stack pointer is active at a time, depending on the operating mode. The stack pointers are designated A7 and A7'. From the designation it should be clear that the active stack pointer can also be addressed as address register 7. Instructions that work with address registers do not address the stack pointer implicitly. Only the currently active stack pointer can be used. One exception to this is the instruction MOVE USP. Since two stacks are present, it is very easy to construct separate stacks for user and supervisor.

The program counter in the 68000 is 32 bits wide. However, only 24 bits are usable via the address bus. The remaining eight bits are intended for later expansion (anticipating such, the 68000 may one day have a 4 gigabyte address space).

Last, but not least is a status register with a width of 16 bits. It is divided into a **user status** (bits 0...7) and a **system status** (bits 8...15). In the user mode, it is only possible to write to the user status. Only the supervisor can change the operating mode of the CPU (which makes sense). The flags tested by conditional branch instructions are found in the user status. The flags give information about the results of many instructions, whether results are zero or negative, if an overflow occurred, etc. A jump to another location in the program can then be made conditional, for instance, on whether or not the previous comparison resulted in zero.

The Registers of the 68000

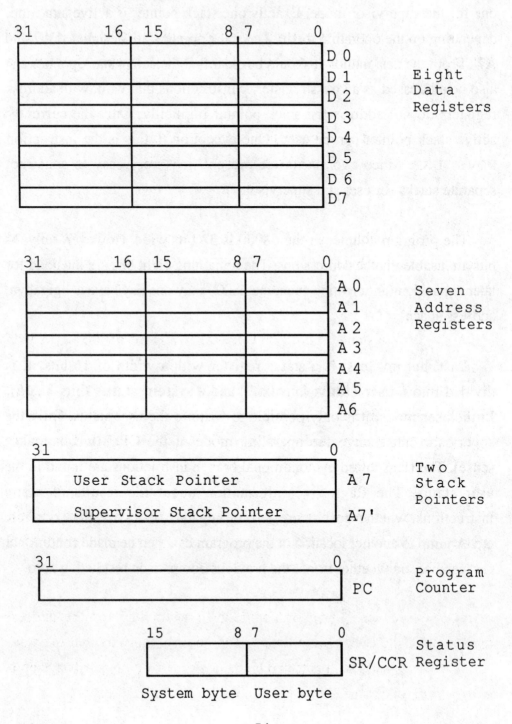

Operand formats

The operand format is either given implicitly by the instruction or is contained explicitly in the instruction. The following operand formats are defined:

1 long word	corresponds to	32 bits
1 word	corresponds to	16 bits
1 byte	corresponds to	8 bits

It is also possible to work with BCD operands. Two BCD digits are "packed" into one byte. In addition to these there are bit manipulation instructions.

A word is the standard operand format, because the 68000 works with a 16-bit data bus.

All operand formats are valid for the data registers. Byte operands occupy the lowest 8 bits, and word operands the lowest 16 bits. Long-word operands use the entire 32 bits.

When a data register is used as a source or destination operand and the operand format is not 32 bits, only the addressed portion of the register is changed. The remainder is neither used nor changed.

Only word and long-word operands are allowed for the address registers and the two stack pointers. The address registers and the stack pointers do not work with byte and bit data. The stack pointers always point to the last valid data and "grow" downward.

When an address register is used as a source operand, either the entire register or just the lower word is used, depending on the operand format selected. If an address register is used as a destination operand, the entire registers is affected, regardless of the operand format. If the format is of a word, all operands are sign-extended to 32 bits.

Status register

The status register consists of a user byte and a system byte.

User byte:

Bit 0 :	Carry flag	Carry	C
Bit 1 :	Overflow flag	Overflow	V
Bit 2 :	Zero flag	Zero	Z
Bit 3 :	Negative flag	Negative	N
Bit 4 :	Extension flag	Extension	X
Bit 5 :	unused	-	
Bit 6 :	unused	-	
Bit 7 :	unused	-	

System byte:

Bit 8..10 :	Interrupt mask	I0, I1, I2
Bit 11 :	unused	-
Bit 12 :	unused	-
Bit 13 :	Supervisor status	-
Bit 14 :	unused	-
Bit 15 :	Trace mode	-

15	14	13	12	11	10	9	8	7	6	5	4	3	2	1	0
T	-	S	-	-	I1	I2	I0	-	-	-	X	N	Z	V	C

Carry

The carry flag is always set to one if an arithmetic operation caused a carry from the highest bit. It is also used to indicate a "borrow" in a subtraction.

Overflow

The overflow flag is used to indicate the user that the number was exceeded during an arithmetic operation. For example, this happens when the result of the addition of two positive numbers does not fit in the register when it represents a two's complement number. The overflow flag is also used for division operations; it indicates that the quotient would be larger than 16 bits, or the dividend is too large.

Zero flag

The zero flag is set if, after an operation, the highest bit of the result is set, indicating that the number is negative in two's complement.

Extension flag

The extension flag behaves just like the carry flag. But it is not affected by all of the instructions influencing the carry flag. For example, it is treated like the carry flag for addition and subtraction, but not for the rotation instructions. The instruction list indicates which instructions affect the extension flag. The extension flag can be used to preserve the carry for multi-byte operations. The extension flag is unique to the 68000.

When reading the other (unused) bits in the user byte of the status register, zero is always returned, even if other values are written to them. This also applies to the status register's unused bits of the system byte. The following terms describe the bits in the system byte:

Interrupt mask

The 68000 has seven interrupt levels (numbered from 1...7). An interrupt is allowed only when the value of the interrupt mask is lower than the priority level of the interrupt. However, interrupt level 7 cannot be disabled; it is what's known as a Non-Maskable Interrupt (NMI). Interrupts can be enabled and disabled by changing the interrupt mask.

Supervisor status

This bit switches the processor between the user and supervisor status. A zero stands for the user status, and a one for the supervisor status. The switch makes it possible to make multi-user systems crash-proof.

Trace-mode

If this bit is set, the 68000 is placed in the trace mode. The 68000 then processes an exception after every instruction. This makes single-step operation of the 68000 in software possible.

Data Organization

Although the 68000 is a 16-bit processor, it works as a byte machine. This means that every word is divided into two bytes and each of these two bytes has its own address. Of course, both bytes of a word can be accessed at once with the 68000, since the data bus is 16 bits wide. Each byte occupies one address in the memory space; each word therefore occupies two addresses. The higher-order byte of the word (the word at address n) is located at the lower address (address n) and the lower-order byte is located at the higher address (address n+1).

The following figures should clarify these concepts:

Byte 000000	Byte 000001	Word 000000
Byte 000002	Byte 000003	Word 000002
Byte 000004	Byte 000005	Word 000004
Byte FFFFFC	Byte FFFFFD	Word FFFFFC
Byte FFFFFE	Byte FFFFFF	Word FFFFFE

Even Address   Odd Address

Bytes and Words in Memory

```
 15      12   11        8 7      4 3        0
┌──────────────────────┬──────────────────────┐
│        Byte 0        │        Byte 1        │  Word n
├──────────────────────┼──────────────────────┤
│        Byte 2        │        Byte 3        │  Word n+2
└──────────────────────┴──────────────────────┘
```

Integer Data (Byte)

```
 15      12   11        8 7      4 3        0
┌─────────────────────────────────────────────┐
│                  Word 0                      │  Word n
├─────────────────────────────────────────────┤
│                  Word 1                      │  Word n+2
├─────────────────────────────────────────────┤
│                  Word 2                      │  Word n+4
└─────────────────────────────────────────────┘
```

Integer Data (Word)

```
 15      12   11        8 7      4 3        0
┌─────────────────────────────────────────────┐
│  Upper Long Word half                        │  Word n
│                        ──Long Word 0──       │
│  Upper Long Word half                        │  Word n+2
├─────────────────────────────────────────────┤
│  Upper long word half                        │  Word n+4
│                        ──Long Word 1──       │
│  Upper long word half                        │  Word n+6
└─────────────────────────────────────────────┘
```

Integer Data (Long Word)

15 12 11 8 7 4 3 0	
BCD 7	BCD 6	BCD 5	BCD 4	Word n
BCD 3	BCD 2	BCD 1	BCD 0	Word n+2

BCD 7 : Highest order digit
BCD 0 : Lowest order digit

Decimal Data (BCD code)

Data Representation

The structure of the 68000 determines some rules for memory access:

1) Access to words and long words are restricted to *even* addresses.

2) This means that operation codes (opcodes or instructions) must be located at *even* addresses.

3) Access to bytes may be at both even *and* odd addresses.

If these rules are not followed, normal operation is interrupted and an exception-handling routine is called by the processor.

Operating states

The 68000 works in either the supervisor mode (supervisor bit = 1) or the user mode (supervisor bit=0). The privileged state determines which operations are allowed. Some instructions are prohibited in the user mode, and if you try to use them, cause an exception. The stack pointer A7' is always used in the supervisor mode, and the stack pointer A7 always used in the user mode. It makes no difference if the stack pointer is used by a instruction implicitly (such as PEA) or if register A7 is specified explicitly as the source or destination in the instruction.

There are three basic operating states of the 68000:

Normal operation

Halt state

Exception handling

The normal execution of instructions represents the first state. A special case of this state is the stopped condition of the CPU. This state is caused by the STOP instruction. No further memory access is possible in this condition.

The halt state is caused by serious errors; should this occur, we must assume that the system is no longer capable of functioning. The processor leaves this state only after an external RESET signal. For example, the halt state is entered when a bus error occurs during the exception handling of a previous bus error (double bus error). However, the halt state is not identical to the stopped condition.

The exception condition results from interrupts, TRAP instructions, the trace operation, or other exception conditions. The implementation of the exception condition makes it possible, for instance, to have the processor react to error situations, or to unforeseen situations.

A peripheral can request the services of the processor through interrupts to process transmitted data.

All exception handling is done in the supervisor mode. When exception handling is begun, the processor saves the old status word on the stack and sets the supervisor bit. All instructions are allowed in the supervisor mode.

The exception handling can be initiated internally or externally. Examples of internal initiation would be address errors (word access to an uneven address), division by zero, direct instructions (TRAP instruction), or the trace mode. Externally, exceptions can be generated by interrupts, bus errors (errors in the bus hardware), or RESET.

The 68000 has a large number of exceptions available, and this is one of its strong points. Through exceptions it is possible to place the processor in the exception state and allow it to react to errors. Here the 68000 surpasses CPUs in many minicomputers, and most other microprocessors.

The individual exception cases are numbered, and the processor fetches an exception vector from memory depending on the case. This vector represents a 32-bit address and it is stored like every other address. The lowest 1024 bytes (or 512 words) of the memory (address space) are used as a table for the 256 vectors.

The status register is saved at the start of the exception handling. The supervisor bit is then set. In addition, the trace bit is cleared, preventing another exception from being generated after the first instruction of the exception handling routine. If an interrupt generated the exception (possible only when the interrupt has a higher priority than the setting in the interrupt mask of the status register), the interrupt mask in the status register is set to the new value. The return address and the old contents of the status register are placed on the supervisor stack.

The processor can receive the vector number in one of two ways. It can create it internally (such as with bus and address errors, but also with auto-vector interrupts); or, it receives the vector number for a non-auto-vector interrupt from the bus (directly or indirectly from the device that generated the interrupt). The 68000 multiplies the vector number by four (by "left-shifting" the bits of the vector number twice). It uses the resulting number as the address. From this address it loads a long-word and into the program counter. Then it begins execution at the instruction to which the (new) program counter points, and so starts to process the exception.

There are 16 special exceptions, called TRAPs, that allow operating system routines in the supervisor mode to be called from user programs running in the user mode. An exception is generated by the instruction "TRAP #n" (with number "n" from 0 to 15). The appropriate operating system functions are then performed in the routine to which the exception vector points. In this manner, it is possible to to make carefully selected calls to program fragments running in the supervisor mode—leaving the protection concept of the 68000 unbroken.

We do not want to delve any deeper into the other individual exceptions, because they are relatively unimportant for learning and understanding machine language.

Addressing modes

The instructions must somehow indicate which operands are to be used. The 68000 instructions consist of two parts:

1) The type of operation to be performed
2) The address of the operand(s)

By address we do not mean only a memory address, since a register can also supply an address.

The instructions can determine the operand address in three ways:

1) Register specification: The register number is given in the instruction.
2) Effective address: Various addressing modes are used to obtain

the address. the selection is made through six bits in the instruction (the 6-bit field is referred to as the effective address).

3) Implicit reference: the operand (a register) is already given in the instuction implicitly.

The 68000 has 14 addressing modes that serve to determine the operand address according to the techniques named. These 14 addressing modes can be divided into six main groups:

Register direct

A register containing the operand is specified directly in the instruction.

Register indirect

A register that contains the address of the operand in memory as specified in the instruction.

Data absolute

The address of the operand in memory is specified explicitly in the instruction.

Relative to program counter

An offset relative to the program counter is given. This means that a signed word or long-word is added to the program counter. The sum is the address of the operand. This addressing mode makes it possible to write programs that can run at any address in the system—programs that are *relocatable*.

Data immediate

The operand is included within the instruction (one or two words).

Implicit

The operand is specified implicitly by the instruction. Stack operations, for example, implicitly have the stack pointer as the pointer to the operand address.

Of the 15 addressing modes, 13 create an effective address. This effective address occupies a field of 2x3 (two times three) bits in the (first) instruction word of the opcode. Additional words required by this immediately follow the first word of the opcode, depending on the addressing mode.

For instructions with effective addresses, the opcode consists of the following:

Bits 0...2:	Contain the register field.
Bits 3...5:	Contain the mode field. (bits 0...5 represent the effective address).
Bits 6...11:	Contain either the effective address of the second operand, or a part of the instruction specification.
Bits 12...15:	Contain the instruction type.

The following table represents the addressing modes that can be selected by an effective address. We use the following abbreviations:

ARI   : Address register indirect

An   : Number of an address register (3 bits, 0..7)

Dn   : Number of a data register (3 bits, 0..7)

Effective address

Mode	Register	Addressing mode
000	Dn	Data register direct
001	An	Address register direct
010	An	Addres register indirect (ARI)
011	An	ARI with post increment
100	An	ARI with predecrement
101	An	ARI with displacement
110	An	ARI with displacement and index
111	000	Absolute short
111	001	Absolute long
111	010	PC relative with displacement
111	011	PC relative with displacement and index
111	100	Data immediate

Effective addressing is not needed for implicit addressing.

The following list explains addressing modes we have not yet described. Their function will become clearer as we use them in program examples.

Address register indirect with post-increment

The address of the operand is found in the address register specified. After the operation, the address register is incremented by 1, 2, or 4, depending on the length of the operand. If the address register is the stack pointer, the address is incremented by at least 2 so that the stack pointer retains an even value. Additional stacks can be constructed with this addressing mode.

Address register indirect with pre-decrement

The specified register is decremented by 1, 2 or 4. If the address register is the stack pointer, it is decremented by 2 or 4 so that it remains even. This prevents address error exceptions. The access is then made to the address which is found in the address register after the subtraction.

Address register indirect with displacement

With this addressing mode, an additonal word is added to the contents of the specified address register. An additional word containing the 16-bit displacement follows the initial. The effective address of the operand is the sum of the register contents and the signed 16-bit address displacement value.

Address register indirect with displacement and index

This addressing mode is analogous to the previous mode. An additional word follows the initial opcode. The lower byte of the additional word represents a signed 8-bit displacement that is added. The upper byte contains information about the type of index register (address or data register), the size of the index (signed word or long-word), and the register number. The effective address is the displacement sum of the register contentsd, the 8-bit displacement and the index register (8- or 16-bits) contents.

Absolute short

An additional word following the initial opcode contains an absolute signed 16-bit address. The effective address is the sum of the register contents and this 16-bit address.

Absolute long

Two additional words follow the initial opcode. The higher-order portion of the 32-bit address is found in the first extension word, and the lower-order portion in the second extension word. The effective address is the sum of the register contents and the 32-bit address.

Program counter (PC) relative with displacement

An additional word is follows the initial opcode containing the 16-bit displacement. The effective address results is the sum of the program counter and this signed 16-bit displacement.

Program counter relative with displacement and index

This addressing mode is analogous to the previous mode. The additional word following the opcode consists of two subfields. The lower byte represents a signed 8-bit displacement that is added to the PC. The upper byte contains information regarding the type of the index register (address or data register), the size of the index (signed word or long word), and the register number. The effective address is the sum of the PC contents, the 8-bit dispalcement and the index register (8- or 16-bits) contents.

Data immediate

One or two additional words follow the initial opcode (depending on the length of the operand) and contain the operand. The lower-order byte of the word is used for byte operations. For long-word operations, the higher-order word is contained in the first word following the initial opcode word and the lower-order in the second word following the opcode.

Overview of the instruction set

The assembly language instruction set of the 68000 is comprised of 56 instructions. This is a small number compared to other processors; however, the 14 addressing modes make the 68000 very flexible and powerful. If each instruction in all addressing modes had its own designation, there would be over 1000 assembler instructions. The 56 instructions can be mastered only because of the open construction of the 68000 with its addressing modes. In addition, the assembly language supports modular programming and, in particular, compiler programming.

The 68000 is a "true" two-address machine. This means that both the source and destination of an operation can reside in memory. This means it is possible to move data from one memory location directly to another. With most other processors, the contents of the memory location must first be moved to a processor register with one instruction, and then written to the other memory location with a second instruction.

A 68000 instruction consists of one to five words, from two to ten bytes. The length and type of the instruction is determined by the first opcode word. The instructions in the 68000 are systematically constructed.

The 68000's instruction set can be divided into the following groups:

- arithmetic operations (with integers)
- BCD instructions
- logical instructions
- shift and rotate instructions
- bit manipulation instructions
- data transfer instructions
- program control instructions

Many 68000 instructions can process several different data types. For example, the MOVE instructions will move bytes, words, and long-words. So in addition to the different addressing modes available for the instructions, different operand lengths are also possible.

Chapter Four

Program and Memory Structures

- Introduction
- Procedures and functions
- Memory structures

Introduction

In early computers, data and program were kept separate from one another. While the data was stored in registers and memory cells, the program was stored from the "outside". Computers were programmed by plug boards in many cases. Another technique of storing the program was to use perforated paper tape.

Present-day digital computers are so-called "Von Neumann computers." We won't bore you with the historical development of the computer. We'll mention only the primary characteristic of a Von Neumann computer: in it the program and the data are stored in the same memory. The central processing unit contains only one register (the program counter) that points to the next executable instruction in the memory. The instructions are simply stored sequentially in memory. By changing the program counter, you can cause the central processor to deviate from the normal sequence of instructions.

This makes jumps in the program possible. You can write programs that react according to the situation while the program is actually running. This is the chief advantage of the Von Neumann computer. In older computers the program runs as a long, single chain of instructions.

In this chapter we present some examples of the construction and structure of programs. You'll find additional examples, especially practical application programs, in later chapters.

One element of conditional structures in programs is the simple **branch**. A branch is made to a certain program part based on a specific condition. If this condition is not fulfilled, execution simply continues with the next instruction in the "instruction chain" (program). As an example, we test to see if the variable A is zero.

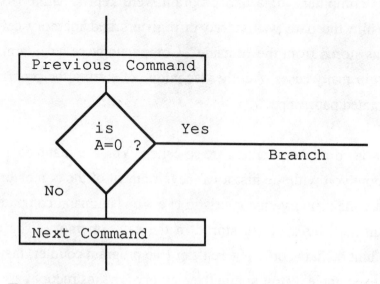

Flow Chart

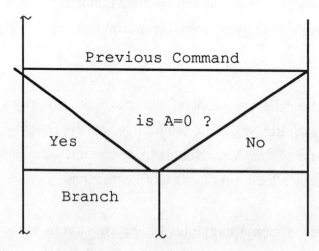

Nassi-Shneiderman Structogram

You must be asking yourself how the execution of the program can continue. We have simply written "branch," but we haven't explained what we meant. Here a specific program part, or segment, is performed only if the condition (A=0) is true. After the execution of that program segment, a branch is usually made back to the main program. Naturally, other branches can be made within the first branch. If the condition is not true, execution simply continues with the next instruction in line. Instead of this, a program segment handling the case of the untrue condition can be called at this point. The program segment called when the condition is true is called the "IF portion"; the other segement is called the "ELSE portion." Here is a short example in Pascal:

```
IF A=0 THEN
         BEGIN
         .   (* Condition is fulfilled *)
         .
         END
      ELSE
         BEGIN
         .   (* Condition is not fulfilled *)
         .
         END;
```

In a BASIC dialect that doesn't have an IF-THEN-ELSE (as opposed to a simple IF-THEN), the algorithm must be formulated differently. For example:

```
10   IF A=0 GOTO 50
20   ...
30   ... (Instructions, if condition not true)
40   GOTO 70
50   ...
60   ... (Instructions, if condition fulfilled)
70   ... (next instruction, same for both)
```

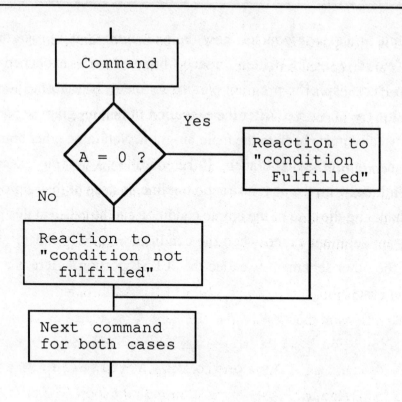

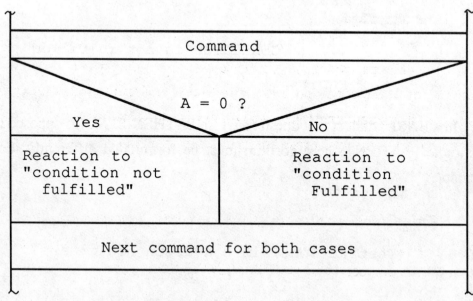

But it is also possible to construct **loops** in programs, in which tests and jumps are executed only when the condition of the test is fulfilled (or not fulfilled). This way we can specify that an action be repeated a certain number of times in succession. There are two different types of loops:

1) The condition is tested before a pass is made through the loop. If the condition is satisfied, the instructions in the loop are executed once and the condition is checked again. If the condition is not satisfied, execution jumps to the program position after the loop.

2) The condition is tested after the actual pass through the loop. The instructions in the loop are therefore always executed at least once. If the condition is satisfied, the next instruction in the program is usually executed. Otherwise execution jumps to the first instruction in the loop. Another "pass" is made through the loop. The condition is then tested again.

With all loops, care must be taken to ensure that they will actually end at some point. If the condition is never fulfilled (as a result of an error in the program) the execution of the loop will never end. This is referred to as the program "hanging up." More reverent programmers call these anomalies "eternal loops."

In many programming languages there are special instructions for constructing loops. As an example, we could print out the multiplication table for the number 4 using a FOR/NEXT loop:

```
10   FOR X = 1 TO 10
20   PRINT 4 * X
30   NEXT X
```

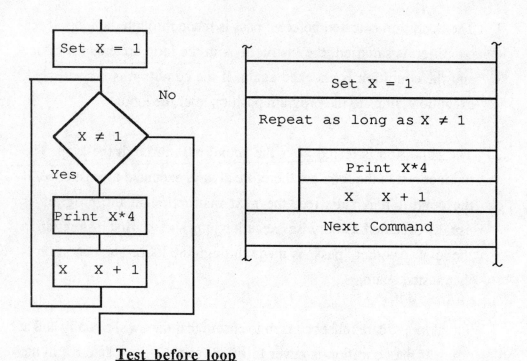

Test before loop

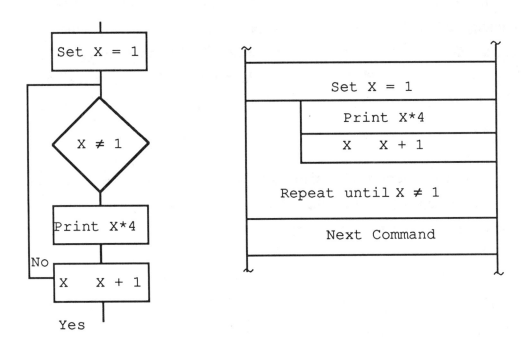

Test after loop

The two drawings show the two basic variants of a loop. The multiplication table for the number 4 is calculated and printed by the programs symbolized there.

In looking at the examples, you can see that in one a test is made for equality, and in the other a test for inequality. In the first example the loops end when the condition is no longer fulfilled. If X reaches the value "11", the loop must be ended. Therefore X is tested to see if it is not equal to 11. If X is no longer *not* equal to 11, then X *is* equal to 11, and the loop is ended.

You can think of many variations of loops all leading to the same result. Try to develop another flowchart. You could, for example, start with X=0 and increment X by one before printing.

There are often loops in which the ending condition is tested in the middle. However, such a loop rarely can be constructed logically. In most cases, the program simply becomes harder to read. In addition, errors often occur, since it is difficult to follow the current value of the index variable (the variable that is changed). For this reason, the index variable should be changed only at the start or end of the loop.

Within a program, a pressed key often initiates some activity. The key pressed is usually stored in a variable. In the program all variants of the variable (the key press) must be tested, and corresponding reactions started. Usually specific procedures or functions are called, dependent on the key pressed. However, a certain program segment often is executed like a "normal" branch.

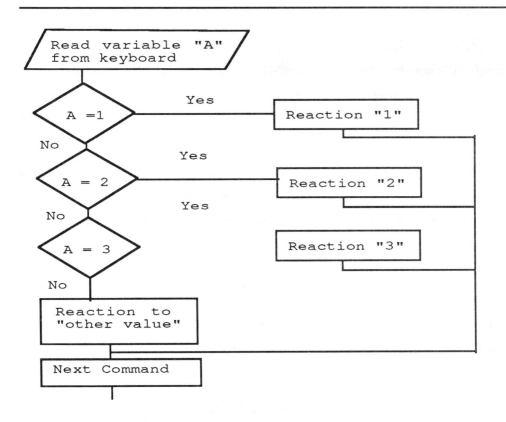

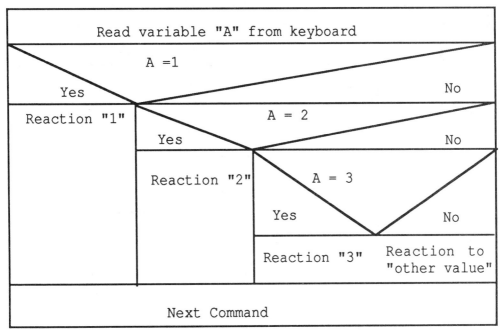

Usually another reaction is defined, a reaction taken if an undefined condition is present (when an invalid key is pressed). We also did this in our example. Another method is to read characters until a valid character is encountered.

As you can see, a Nassi-Shneiderman structogram can become difficult to read very quickly. Consequently, it is very difficult or impossible to use when creating the program on the computer. But there is another way to draw structograms. The second method avoids using the triangle for tests. In addition, the individual variables are listed under each other and not next to each other, so that such structograms can be written with "normal" word processing programs. This is an important advantage srtuctograms have over flowcharts. Here is our last example, written differently:

```
┌─────────────────────────────────────────────────────────────┐
│ A is read from keyboard                                      │
├─────────────────────────────────────────────────────────────┤
│ Is A = 1                                                     │
│          ┌──────────────────────────────────────────────────┤
│ Yes      │ Reaction 1                                        │
│          ├──────────────────────────────────────────────────┤
│          │ Is A = 2                                          │
│          │         ┌────────────────────────────────────────┤
│ No       │ Yes     │ Reaction 2                              │
│          │         ├────────────────────────────────────────┤
│          │ No      │ Is A = 3                                │
│          │         │         ┌──────────────────────────────┤
│          │         │ Yes     │ Reaction 3                    │
│          │         │         ├──────────────────────────────┤
│          │         │ No      │ Reaction other A              │
├──────────┴─────────┴─────────┴──────────────────────────────┤
│ Next command                                                 │
└─────────────────────────────────────────────────────────────┘
```

84

There are also other techniques for clearly representing structograms. The example we selected has the disadvantage of requiring a wide work sheet for "nested" tests. For learning machine language, the structogram we selected and the Nassi-Shneiderman will work well. Flowcharts are also good for this purpose; their major disadvantage is that they can easily create spaghetti code, because they do not force structured programming. It may not be clear now why small programs have to be programmed "cleanly," but it's a good idea to learn and practice the techniques for larger programs. We will go into some structured programming approaches in the next section.

Procedures and functions

Clearly we can write very capable programs with the different tests, branches, and loops. But in practice it often occurs that a certain program segment is needed at different locations. Here it usually doesn't make sense to repeat the same program text in all the places it's required.

The technique of **subroutine** was devised for just this purpose. You already know of these from BASIC; they work much the same way in machine language. An example is shown on the next page.

```
 10  ...         (program)
 20  GOSUB 100   (subroutine call)
 30  ...         (first command after the subroutine)
100  ...         (start of subroutine)
110  ...         (subroutine)
120  RETURN      (return to the calling program)
```

A subroutine call is like a normal jump to another place in the program. But in a subroutine call, the address of the next command after the subroutine call is placed on the system stack (we will explain what we mean by this later). As soon as the CPU gets the command to return from the subroutine, it gets the address from the system stack and thereby knows exactly where it has to jump.

The return addresses can be simply stored on the system stack when several calls are nested within each other—i.e. when one subroutine calls another. When returning, the processor always reads the top address off the stack, and the other data on the stack is "pulled" toward the top of the stack.

The disadvantage of this procedure is that no parameters can be passed directly to the subroutine. In addition, the subroutine cannot pass any value back directly to the caller.

Efficient programs can be written even with this disadvantage. Problems will always arise when the subroutine of one program is used in another program. In addition, programs written in this manner are almost always hard to read because the parameters, etc., can be difficult to follow. Moreover, leapfrogging all over the place will produce more spaghetti code; however, in practice, the exclusive use of subroutine calls and returns is rare.

Subroutines can be defined differently, however. In Pascal (and also in other languages like ADA, Modula 2, C, etc.), there are structures known as **procedures** and **functions**. A function or procedure is called like a normal subroutine. But as part of the call, the pre-defined parameters are passed to the subroutine. These parameters are stored in the subroutine as local variables. They are variables that can be used only by the subroutine, and are usually erased when execution returns to the main program. This way, even errors resulting from the improper use of variables in large programs can be avoided. Above all, procedures and functions can be easily used in other programs.

When the procedure or function is ended, control is returned to the main program as with simple subroutines. This causes the local variables (the variables used only by the subroutine) to be erased. With a function, a value—known as the function value—is also returned to the calling program. Herein lies the difference between a procedure and a function—a function always returns a value. Naturally, groups of values can also serve as the function value. The function value can be viewed as the "result" of the function.

Next we present a typical function and a typical procedure, both formulated in Pascal. Example:

```
FUNCTION SQUARE (X: REAL) : REAL;
      BEGIN
        SQUARE := X*X;
      END;
```

This function calculates the square of a number. The expression SQUARE(9) returns "81", for example.

The next example is a procedure that outputs a given number of blank lines. The expression LINE(10) will write 10 blank lines:

```
PROCEDURE LINE(N: INT);
     VAR I: INT;
     BEGIN
       FOR I:=1 TO N DO
          WRITELN;
     END;
```

The machine language of the 68000, like that of other processors, is not fully implemented. For the most part only instructions to initiate a subroutine call and return from the subroutine are present. But the 68000 has an advantage over other processors in that it has instructions that reserve and free memory for local variables. Therefore, in order to be able to work with procedures and functions in machine language, you must create a **procedure convention.**

A procedure convention is an agreement; it's a statement of intent as to how parameters will be passed to the subroutine, and how function values will be returned. In addition, a procedure convention usually determines which registers retain their old values when the subroutine returns. In chapter 7 we'll present the procedure convention used in this book's examples.

Memory Structures

In the second chapter we mentioned that, from the point of view of the software, the memory is linear, or one-dimensional. The memory appears as an array of bytes, each byte having its own address. In hardware, bytes are paired together, because the 68000 is a 16-bit processor. Access is usually made only to even-numbered addresses for this reason. But the 68000 need perform only one read or write cycle for a word access.

In practice, multi-dimensional arrays are needed more often than one-dimensional memory. Appropriate software can accomplish this easily.

To do this, the size of the array must be limited. The multi-dimensional array can then be structured in the available memory. The following can be done for a two-dimensional array with $100 X $100 (256 * 256) elements, each one byte large; assume that the array will begin at address $10000. Then the individual rows of the field begin at the following addresses:

Row $0   : $10000..$100FF

Row $1   : $10100..$101FF

Row $2   : $10200..$102FF

.   .

.   .

Row $FE : $1FE00..$1FEFF

Row $FF : $1FF00..$1FFFF

Element $30 in row $2 would then be located at address $10230. Arrays of higher dimension can be defined according to the same principle. You must ensure that the border of a row is never exceeded, since this is equivalent to accessing a different row.

In the last section we use a **stack** to store return addresses. But what do we mean by a stack?

Another designation for stack is a LIFO structure. LIFO being an acronym for Last-In First-Out. This name already defines the operation of a stack quite well. The data last placed on the stack is the first to be read back out. We can compare a stack in memory to a stack of papers. New information is written on a sheet of paper and placed on the top of the stack. If information is required, the last piece of paper placed on the stack is the first to be removed.

In practice, a stack works like this:

A certain memory area is reserved for the stack. A CPU register, called the stack pointer, points to a word in this memory area. If data is placed on the stack, the stack pointer is simply decremented by the number of bytes to be written. The data is written in the address range between the old and new stack pointer values. Reading data from the stack is also simple. The contents of the memory location to which the stack pointer points are read. The data on the stack is no longer available and is made "invalid" by incrementing the stack pointer by the number of bytes read.

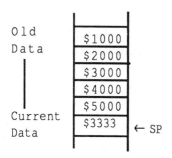

Principle of a Stack on the 68000

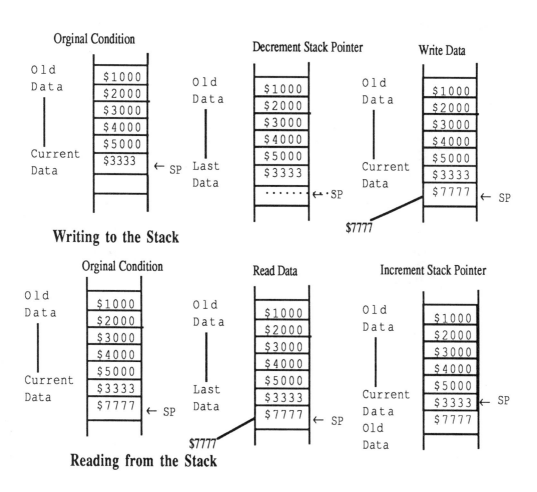

Writing to the Stack

Reading from the Stack

Operation of the Stack on the 68000

In the 68000, address register A7 (or A7' in the supervisor mode) is defined as the **system stack pointer**. It is automatically used for subroutine calls, such as those made using JSR, for storing the return address. Other instructions also use A7 (or A7') as the stack pointer implicitly. But all of the other address registers can also be used as stack pointers for user stacks, using the addressing modes "address register indirect with predecrement" and "address register indirect with postdecrement."

The use of the stack pointer is implemented on the 68000 as follows:

1) The stack pointer always points to the current entry—the entry at the very top of the stack.

2) The stack "grows" downward, to lower addresses. The stack pointer is therefore decremented every time new entries are placed on the stack; it is incremented every time entries are removed from it.

In the context of this definition, data that is physically "lower" in memory is logically "higher" on the stack. This is somewhat confusing; but its meaning should become clearer as we begin to work with stacks.

Something called FIFO storage is often used to store data temporarily; FIFO is an acronym for First-In First-Out. Commonly called a buffer, FIFO storage can be used in data transfer programs, for example. It often occurs that the receiver returns the data at regular intervals, but the receiving program can't always process it immediately. Instead, it saves data on the disk from time to time. In this situation you can program the data transfer with a buffer storage. Each time a byte is received, the processor interrupts its normal activity and places the byte from the receiver in the buffer storage. The main program then always gets the data from the buffer when it is required.

Naturally, certain problems can arise, because buffers have finite memory area. You must ensure that the data is processed quickly enough. Also, the data must be stored in the buffer almost immediately—otherwise new data may arrive while the current data is being stored, and data will be lost.

A practical problem results from the principle of the FIFO storage/buffers. A stack grows in one direction, but it is always built "from the top." One byte in the stack memory area is used again and again. In a buffer, each byte is used only once. After this, the "chain" of data has moved on by one position.

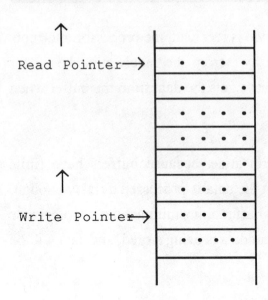

<u>FIFO Storage</u>

In practice, buffers generally are built as ring storage. Ring storage can be imagined simply as a ring, or circle, of bytes. Each of these bytes has a certain address. There are also two pointers, one for write and one for read, that are required by the ring. The write pointer always points to the address to which the next write access will go; after the write, it is incremented by the number of bytes written. The read pointer points to the location at which the reader (the program or programs that fetch the data from the buffer) can find the next byte. After a byte is read, this pointer is also incremented.

One error situation can occur using this structure. If the reader and writer operate at markedly different speeds, one may catch up to the other. Therefore, when changing the value of one pointer, it's necessary to check the value of the other pointer.

You will no doubt ask yourself how a ring buffer can be made out of linear memory. To do it, an area of memory is designated as ring storage (FIFO storage). Once the read or write pointer reaches the highest address in the storage area, it is reset to the starting address of the buffer on the next increment. This requires another test when changing the pointer. Moreover, a situation will arise where the value of the write pointer is lower than that of the read pointer. But according to the principle of a buffer, the position where writing will take place is *after* the read position. The comparisons required to detect errors in the pointer values are not all that easy to formulate.

Chapter Five

Operating System and Programs

Introduction

Any microcomputer requires a program to do useful work. When the 68000 is sitting idle with no devices interrupting the system bus, it tries to execute the next instruction. The 68000 can be put in a "sleep" state wherein it waits for an interupt, and is otherwise inactive. This state is generated by the STOP instruction, and is called the "halt" state. If, during the operation of the 68000, serious errors occur and it is determined that reasonable operation can no longer continue (such as a double bus error), the halt state is entered. This can be exited only through a processor RESET.

Since a microprocessor cannot function without a program, a program is required as soon as the computer is turned on. This program reads the instructions and determines what it will do next. On many computers, the built-in BASIC interpreter (or other programming language) is simply started after the computer is turned on. Larger systems, particularly systems with disk drives, generally have more complex system software.

Some tasks must be performed in every program. Almost every program requires character input/output via the keyboard, screen, and printer. In addition, all programs are required to read from and write to the disk drive in the same way, so that a diskette can hold multiple programs and data. It doesn't make any sense to rewrite the necessary routines (subroutines or procedures and functions) in every program. This is why almost all computers have what is known as an **operating system**.

The operating system contains the routines required to operate the peripherals. The programs are usually divided into machine-dependent and machine-independent parts. If the operating system is to be used on other computers (ported), then only the machine-dependent parts need be rewritten or changed for the new computer.

The actual user programs (such as word processors or BASIC) then access the peripherals via the operating system. Since the operating system can be the same on different computers, programs can be run on different computers without any changes; as a result, computers with the same operating system but different hardware can be interchanged.

Large operating systems often have the task of managing the working memory. Programs request the required working memory from the operating system.

The actual user does not come into contact with the heart of the operating system, as long as he does not write any programs on the operating system level. Another part of the operating system is the user level. To the user level belong programs with which the user can tell the operating system to execute a program, to erase files from the diskette, print them out, and so on.

On the Atari ST, the TOS operating system is used with the GEM interface for the user. TOS is in many respects identical to CP/M68K from Digital Research. It offers routines for accessing the peripherals. Control of screen windows, the use of the mouse, and so on are all controlled by GEM. We won't go any further into the structure of TOS and GEM, but will explain their operation as far as necessary in the following chapters.

Up to now we have assumed that the computer executes only one program. But there are operating systems that allow the computer to appear to execute several programs simultaneously. Such operating systems are called mulit-tasking operating systems. By simultaneous we mean that the computer executes one program for a fraction of second, and then executes the next one for a fraction, switching back and forth, switching back and forth. This procedure is usually called time-sharing.

Multi-tasking can be performed in one of two ways:

1)   A program runs in the *foreground*. The user works with the program interactively. All other programs run in the *background*. After a background program has been started, it runs on its own without further accessing the screen or keyboard. For example, a background program can print a file to the printer, while a processor interacts with the user in the foreground.

2)   There is no distinction made between foreground and background. The screen can be switched from one task or program to another by means of a simple command. A new window can be opened for a new task. This technique is considerably easier to use than the first, but requires a considerably more complicated operating system. But this actually allows use of two programs at once.

With multi-tasking you can do more than execute various programs on the user level at the same time. Individual programs could be composed of different programs. A word processing program could consist two parts. The first part would be a conventional word processing program; the second could be a program that at regular intervals made backup copies of text being edited. Since both programs run at the same time, the user isn't even aware that the backup is being made.

Multiple "terminals" (screen and keyboard) can also be serviced with a single microprocessor. Just as a multi-tasking operating system (of the second type) executes multiple programs simultaneously on one terminal, an operating system can also execute multiple programs on multiple terminals. In this manner, several users can work on one computer at the same time. Systems using this technique are called multi-user systems.

Programs

A microprocessor works only with its machine language. It does not understand high-level programming languages (although there are processors with a built-in programming language, such as FORTH or BASIC). The machine language is simply a stream of bits that represent the instructions and immediate data of a program. It is difficult for humans to read, since there are no readily apparent connections between the machine language instruction and the resulting code. Programming languages were created because of the very fact that machine language is difficult to read. "High-level" language programs can be converted to machine language by appropriate programs.

Additional utility programs are used to write the program text, and to test and correct the software. We would like to present a few groups of these programs in order to clarify the terms.

Assembler

Every machine language instruction is assigned a mnemonic by the manufacturer of the microprocessor. The assembler translates the mnemonics into the machine language. For example, since jumps are possible only to addresses, and it is not yet clear when writing the program where sections of the program will end up in memory, the assember also inserts the proper addresses. The programmer puts labels in the program to indicate jump destinations. In addition, names can be given to memory locations. These memory locations can then be used like variables. Here is a fragment of an example assembly language program:

```
addbcd:     MOVEA.L     #SOURCEPTR,A0
            MOVEA.L     #DESTPTR,A1
            MOVE.W      #length-1,D0
addloop:    ABCD        -(A0),-(A1)
            DBF         D0,addloop
```

In the final analysis, writing programs in assembly language is equivalent to writing them in machine language. But the assembler syntax is mastered much more easily than the cryptic bit streams of the machine language itself, because the mnemonics represent "abbreviations" of the instructions.

Compiler

A compiler is a program that translates programs in a "high-level" programming language into machine language. For instance, Pascal is converted to machine language by means of a compiler. Compilers and assemblers are based on the same principle. The difference is that a compiler usually converts a high-level language command into

103

several machine language instructions. An assembler, on the other hand, translates each assembly language instruction into exactly *one* machine language instruction. Various checks are made while the programming is running, depending on the language. In Pascal, for example, the array bounds may be checked for a valid range. By contrast, almost no checks are made in C. This makes C programs faster than Pascal programs but significant errors can easily occur.

Interpreter

An interpreter does not convert a high-level language program. Instead, the interpreter executes an equivalent sequence of machine language instructions for each command in the high-level language. A single command is read, interpreted, and executed. A command in a loop that's executed 100 times is completely read, interpreted and executed 100 times. The advantage of an interpreter is that the entire program need not be retranslated after making a change in the test phase.

In practice, often it's hard to tell compilers from interpreters. For example, there are Pascal compilers (such as UCSD Pascal) that do not compile to machine language, but to a pseudo-code. This pseudo-code resembles machine language, but must be executed by an interpreter.

Editor

An editor is a program that writes text for programming languages. In many programming languages (like BASIC), the editor is already included as part of the programming language. For others (like Pascal and C), a separate editor is used. A wordprocessing program is an editor intended not for programs but for letters, books, and so on. This book was written using a word processing program.

Monitor

A monitor is a program allowing us to view and change memory locations and processor registers directly. In addition, a monitor has functions to convert machine language back into mnemonics (to "disassemble" it). A monitor program is usually used to check and test as well as correct programs in machine language.

Debugger

A monitor is also a debugger. A debugger is a program that aids in finding program errors. There are not only debuggers that work on the machine language level like a monitor, but also those that work directly with a high-level language.

Linker

A linker is a program that combines multiple, individually assembled machine language program segments. Modules of different languages can also be combined with a linker. For example, speed-critical program fragments written in assembler are often combined with Pascal programs.

There are many other tools available to the programmer in addition to the programs named here. For example, the Atari ST development system has a program that lets you easily develop the icons that symbolize the files. Other tools create lists of the variables used in a program.

Chapter Six

Fundamentals of Assembly Language Programming

- •Introduction

- •The editor

- •The assembler

- •The debugger

- •Procedure conventions

Introduction

In this chapter we want to familiarize ourselves with the functions of a 68000 assembler. We'll explain important terms used in assembly language programming and introduce the assembler's general operation and special syntactical rules. We want to prepare you for assembly language programming by showing you the full range of features.

The authors used the assembler included with the Atari 520 ST Development System.

The Atari Development System contains the CP/M 68K assembler (AS68) from Digital Research. You do not need an assembler in order to understand the examples in this book. However, if you want to write your own programs in assembly language, some kind of assembler is required.

The editor

Up until now we have always spoken of a program as an abtsract representation of instructions that the assembler translates into machine language instructions. These instructions resemble a language—the programming language. All programs formulated in languages are represented in some written form. This written form is the **program text**.

The program text must, like every written document, be entered into the computer by the programmer before it can be processed. A special program is required to do this—the **editor**.

The program text is stored on the diskette/hard disk as a **file**. The editor is in control of all the possibilities for creating and changing a text file. The ease with which these functions can be used depends on the editor.

An editor called MINCE was used with the Atari ST Development System. In principle, any editor that creates text files in ASCII code can be used for entering a program. Therefore it is possible to use an editor that is not included with the assembler. This makes sense if you have an editor that exceeds the capabilities of the assembler editor, or if you just want to use a single editor.

The list on the next page should give you an idea of an editor's tasks.

- Create a text file on the diskette/hard disk
- Modify a test file
- Delete a text file from the diskette/hard disk
- Accept characters from the keyboard
- Display the text on the screen
- Output a text on the printer
- Execute an editor command
- Move text on the screen
- Format the text

As a general rule, the editor is started from the operating system level (GEM or TOS). The file to be processed is identified or named when the editor is started. If the file already exists, the editor loads the file from the diskette/hard disk into memory and displays it on the screen. If the file is new, a new text file is created. In addition to the text you're currently working on, the editor displays additional information about the text.

This additional information includes statements about the amount of memory available for additional text, descriptions of the currently available editor functions, information such as the position of the cursor (page/line/column), and the name of the file being edited.

Once the editor is started and a file is being processed (even a new, previous empty text), the programmer is in the edit mode of the editor. On this level the editor has three basic operating modes: **Writing** mode, **Movement** mode, and **Command** mode.

In the Writing mode, all letters, digits, and special characters entered are inserted into the text. The Writing mode is automatically selected by pressing an appropriate key. A character entered always appears at the current cursor position.

By using the cursor keys, the cursor position in the text can be changed. The editor is automatically placed in the Movement mode when an appropriate cursor key is pressed.

As a rule, the Command mode is activated by pressing the control key together with a letter key. One or more of these key combinations cause the editor to execute a certain command. There are both simple and very complex commands that make text processing flexible and complete.

Here's an overview of the more popular editor commands:

Write mode: Digits, letters, special characters

Movement mode: Cursor left, right, up, down
                             Delete character (delete, backspace)
                             Tab

Command mode:

  •File management: Read, write, delete file
                             Save (write, continue)
                             Rename, copy file
                             Display disk contents
                             Insert text block (from disk)

•Movement: Word left, word right

Start of line, start of new line

Line forewards, line backwards

Page forewards, page backwards

Start of text, end of text

•Delete: Word left, word right

From start of line to cursor

From cursor to end of line

From cursor to end of text

Delete line

Delete entire text

•Block commands: Mark start of block

Mark end of block

Delete marked block

Copy marked block

Move marked block

Save marked block (disk)

•Other: Search in text

Search and replace

Print text file

Set or clear tabs

End program and save text

Interrupt program

Call help text

The assembler

The term **assembler** is used to refer to a collection of programs that allow the programmer to work with machine language on the computer. An assembler program package has several distinct functions, and typically includes an editor and a debugger.

In this section we'll discuss the typical components of an assembler package such as the debugger. But first let's take a look at the actual assembler. When we speak of an assembler, we refer to a program that takes machine language instructions written in symbolic form and stored as a text file, and translates them into codes that the 68000 processor can execute.

Operation of the assembler

As you already know, an assembler is just a program that processes data according to certain rules. The data to be processed is a series of symbolic machine language commands (mnemonics). These instructions comprise a file that is typically entered into the computer using an editor and saved as a text file on diskette or hard disk for later processing. Since the assembler creates a machine language program from this text file, it is often designated as the **source file**, or **source text**.

The goal of processing a source file is to create an executable machine language program. Since this translation procedure is peformed by the assembler, this process is also called assembly or assembling.

As a general rule, the resulting code of an assembly is stored on the disk, again in the form of a file. Since a finished machine language program represents only a specific arrangement of binary data, this file is called a **binary file**. Other names used for it are object file, object code, absolute file and destination file. It should be mentioned that an assembler can also manage the source and destination files directly in the memory of the computer. This is called memory-to-memory assembly. This has its advantages when you're working with short programs and/or on small computers, in that processing speed is increased considerably because no mass storage accesses are required for the assembly.

For computer systems with the performance features of the Atari ST, a good assembler offers the capability of creating relocatable files. In contrast to executable machine language programs (which, as a rule, are bound to a specific address space in the computer's memory), a relocatable file consists of a "half-finished" machine language program missing the address space specifications for the address space. These address specifications are stored in a special way in a relocatable file. To create an executable machine language program from a relocatable file, a special utility program is needed to combine the "half-finished" conversion with the address specifications or location. This creates an executable binary file from the machine language program, or it loads the machine language program into memory at the same time. Such a utility program is called a **loader**.

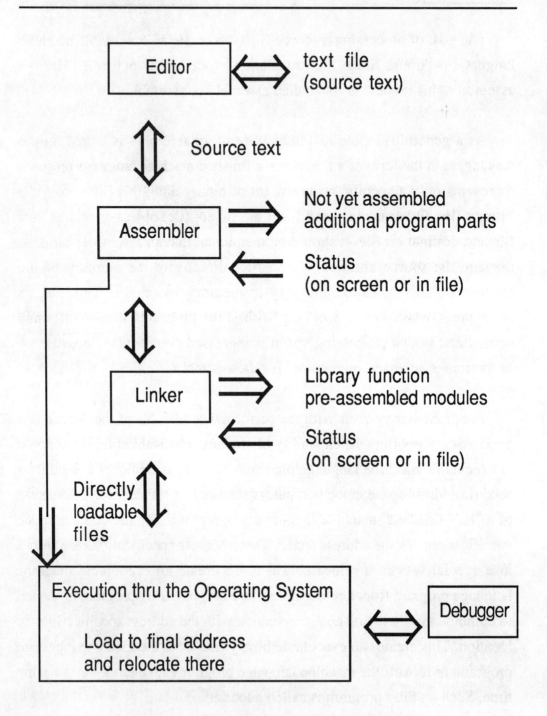

Overview of assembly language programming

At first, working with relocatable files sounds complicated, but it offers enormous advantages when considered and used carefully. Since the loader must insert absolute addresses in the half-finished machine code, it performs its task considerably faster than a complete assembly. The loader does not have to make any conversions or error checks, because these were all made by the assembler. Individual machine language programs are usually created in a relocatable form when a program must be loaded at different addresses. This is often the case during the test phase of a program. As an alternative to using a loader, the programmer can write his programs using relocatable code, in which no absolute addressing is used.

But there are also other, more significant aspects of relocatable files. By using another utility program—the **linker**—you can combine several separately assembled, relocatable files into a single program. A new binary or relocatable file then can be created by a linker.

You can use the combination of relocatable files and the linker for many purposes. When you create larger programs, you will probably divide the whole program into several small, logically distinct program modules. These smaller programs can be developed and tested separately. When some of the parts are finished, you can combine these modules into larger modules and test it again until you have finished the program.

Working this way, you will discover modules that were running smoothly suddenly behave wildly when you add a new module. If you are working with a single source text in such cases, you must reassemble the entire file for each test pass—even the parts already working. This wastes time unnecessarily. It is much better to break large programs up into smaller source files and relocatable files. In the test phase you will have to make changes to and reassemble only the suspect module. You then can quickly create an executable program with the linker.

This modularization has some interesting side effects. For example, when working with large, complex programs, you can store the source files of finished modules on another disk, keeping only the relocatable files on the work diskette. This saves space on the disk that you can use for your current source files. From experience, we have found that the ratio of the source file size to the size of the resulting machine language program is about 10 to 1. If you write programs as collections of individual modules, using sensible divisions and standard procedure conventions (which we'll talk about later), over time you will develop an entire collection of library functions that you can use in new programs.

We should mention here that there are several such complete, tested libraries on the market. There are, for example, comprehensive libraries for file management or for solving special numerical problems. A professional programmer can become considerably more efficient by using the routines contained in such libraries.

Another important application of relocatable files is when we want to solve some special problems in machine language, but actually write the main program in a compiled language. The problem lies in connecting the program parts written in machine language to those that the compiler converted to machine language itself. As a general rule, compilers can also be instructed to create relocatable files. The linker can then combine these files with your own machine language programs. This lets you design programs consisting of modules created by different high-level language compilers.

Let us now turn briefly to another possible component of the assembler package. Often a debugger or a monitor is used during the development and test phase. When looking for errors, we can view the machine language program directly in memory, and perhaps modify it for test purposes.

The debugger or monitor is a component of most development packages. Since the debugger or monitor displays your assembled machine language program, it is unaware of the source file from which the assembled code was produced. It cannot give you any information about the variable names that you used in in the source file, for example. Therefore the debugger or monitor becomes less and less useful, unless the programmer can remember what variables the machine code represents.

To address this shortcoming, many assembler packages use **symbol files** or **label files**. This file contains all of the symbolic names that the programmer defined in high-level language. In addition, the assembler places information in this symbol file corresponding to the absolute values of these symbols. When using a relocatable file, the symbol file is naturally expanded by the linker. This makes all of the important information available, separate from the executable machine language program. The debugger or monitor can display the complete information about the machine language program at any time by evaluating the symbol table. Some systems even make the entire source text with all of the programmer's comments available.

In conclusion, we would like to mention that the assembler also creates a listing as it assembles. This listing contains the source file and machine language opcodes produced by the assembler. This is very useful in the test phase, when the assembler also creates a **symbol table**. All of the variable names (symbols) defined by the programmer, and together with their assigned values are listed (and usually sorted) in the symbol table. A cross reference list (or simply **cross reference**) showing all program lines where the variables were found is also produced by most assemblers.

Short assembler typology

Here we would like to take the time to clarify some important differences between various assembler packages. If you are considering purchasing an assembler, you should familiarize yourself with the various features so that you can make the right purchase decision.

The simplest form of an assembler is the **direct assembler**, or line-by-line assembler. For this form of assembler there is no source file and no editor. The programmer interacts with the assembler. He enters a single instruction directly to the assembler. The assembler then immediately translates the entire line into the corresponding machine code, and also places the result directly into memory. This type of assembler does not work with symbols. A line-by-line assembler rarely forms the heart of an assembler package. But it is a useful tool within a monitor or debugger, allowing quick changes to a machine language program being tested without having to use the actual assembler. It doesn't make sense to use a line-by-line assembler for long programs.

For more comprehensive programs a full **symbolic assembler** may be used. This type of assembler allows the use of symbolic names for constants, variables, and addresses in the source file. We'll explore the flexibility that symbols offer later in the book. Here we'll say only that a symbolic assembler performs two passes through a source file in order to create a machine language program. During the first pass the assembler searches the source file looking for symbols and creates the values of these symbols. The machine language code is generated during the second pass. Because of this characteristic, this type is also known as a two-pass assembler. Some assemblers use additional passes when assembling.

A **macroassembler** offers even more capabilities and options. A macro is a sequence of several machine language instructions that can be defined by the programmer with a macro name. Macros are usually defined for recurring sequences of instructions in the source text. Wherever the programmer puts a macro call in the source text, it behaves as if the programmer had actually typed in all of the instructions for which the macro stands. You can define an entire library of typical instruction sequences with macros. Since this is not a programming technique *per se*, macro processing is also known as pure text substitution, a sort of programming shorthand.

For the sake of thoroughness, and to prevent confusion of terms, we'll mention the term **cross assembler**. An assembler does not necessarily have to be implemented on the machine for which it creates machine code. The computer on which the cross assembler runs is called the host. The computer on which the generated machine code is to run is called the target. Machine code produced by a cross assembler usually cannot be run on the host computers. Testing machine language program under such conditions calls for a simulation program. Cross assemblers are mainly used in cases where the target system does not exist yet (computers in development) or the target system is not powerful enough to support program development (microcontrollers).

The format of the source file

As we have already learned, a source file represents the symbolic form of a machine language program. The text of the source file is line-oriented, whereby each line usually contains just one instruction that the assembler processes. The logical processing sequence within a line is from left to right, from the first (top) line to the last (bottom). This form of representation follows our normal style of reading written materials, i.e. newspapers, books, etc.

In an assembly language program, we can distinguish between several groups of instructions that perform certain tasks, and their different syntactic rules. In this section we want to familiarize you with these groups of instructions before we discuss them individually.

As already mentioned, in an assembly language program, machine language instructions are represented by mnemonics and operands. A label may be placed in front of a mnemonic and is a symbol designation of the address at which a machine language instruction is created by the assembler. The programmer may use this label to refer to this address elsewhere in the program without having to know the value of the address. We'll discuss symbols in more detail later.

A line within the source file may also contain a **comment.** Comments explain the purpose of complex programs and the programmer may make the algorithms that he uses easier to understand. We recommend that you place comments within the source files so that it is clear what it going on in the program. Naturally, a line within a source file may contain only a label and/or comment. This serves only to improve the readability and appearance of the program text and has no other function. We can include these lines in a source file, even though they create no machine code. The same applies to blank lines.

Another group of assembler instructions includes all types of direct label and symbol definitions. These lines are called **declarations**. Other terms that you may encounter are value assignments and symbol or address definitions.

A declaration is the assignment of a specific value to a symbol or label. Declarations are used by the programmer to keep a program independent of values as much as possible. For example, a programmer can designate a print position as "column" and assign the constant "10" to this designation. In the program he can always refer to the symbol "column" when he means the print position "10". This has two useful effects. First, the self-documenting nature of the program is increased; second, the program becomes easier to change. If the programmer wants to change the print position later, he need change only the constant in the declaration of the symbol "column". The assembler then uses the new print position wherever the symbol "column" appears.

We have already mentioned labels. In contrast to symbols, which designate variable and constant values, labels are used exclusively for the symbolic designation of addresses. Not every address used by the programmer (jump destinations in particular) can be defined by a label in a line of source code. This is because some of these jump destinations do not lie within the assembly language program. These addresses, which must be defined by means of a symbol declaration, are designated as external labels.

Some assemblers are capable of textual declarations. Special reserved symbol names are assigned text strings. Such a textual declaration could be, for example, "D0 = COUNTER". "D0" is a reserved symbol and in the assembler syntax designates a data register of the 68000. If the programmer uses this declaration in his/her program, the assembler understands from this declaration that the programmer wants to refer to the D0 register as "COUNTER". This function also has no effect on the logical operation of the machine language program. Good programmers often write their programs completely symbolically, as this practice leads to fewer errors.

The last group of assembly language instructions is the **assembler directives**. These are often referred to as pseudo-opcodes, or simply pseudo-ops. As a general rule, assembler directives do not create machine code. They serve to control the assembly, to select certain options, and to organize the machine instructions in memory. We can divide the directives into various groups according to their function. The most important directive in assembly language programming tells the assembler where the assembled code will reside in memory. In this same group are all the directives that tell the assembler where in memory it should reserve space for data, or where tables will be defined. Other directives are responsible for the appearance of the listing or telling the assembler what source files it should work with. More on this later.

Constants and arithmetic expressions

In assembly language programming, we distinguish only between numeric and alphanumeric constants. As you have already learned, microprocessors work with binary data. Numerical constants can be represented in various number systems according to the purpose they serve. Syntax rules governing the designation of the number system make it possible for the assembler to interpret a constant in a specific number system.

In the decimal system, numbers are represented by the digits 0-9. In some cases, a "#" (number sign) is placed in front of the decimal number.

Examples: 100
             #100

Some assemblers recognize hexadecimal numbers by default. To distinguish hexadecimal numbers from decimal numbers and symbols, they must have a leading zero. This is often the case, because a programmer almost always writes hex numbers in byte or word form. Another possibility is to precede the number with a "$" (as we have used) or suffix the number with the letter "H".

Examples: 0D
            $F000
            1000H

Some assemblers also allow the representation of octal numbers. Octal numbers are usually indicated with an "@" sign placed before or after the number.

Examples: 17@

              @10

You can also represent binary numbers; they are indicated with a "%" placed before or after the number.

Examples: %1000000

              %1010

Independent of the representation and the number of places specified, the assembler evaluates numbers from the right. It automatically expands or truncates the number to fit the appropriate size of the operand. If bits are lost during this process, a warning message is usually indicated.

Some assemblers allow the use of a variable number base. Here the number is followed by an "X" and the number base. The number base is specified in decimal.

Examples: 1010x2   (binary number)   corresponds to decimal 10

            1000x8   (octal number)   corresponds to decimal 512

            1250x10 (decimal number) corresponds to decimal 1250

            2000x16 (hex number)   corresponds to decimal 8192

An **alphanumeric** constant is designated as a sequence of characters in ASCII code. It doesn't matter if the codes are printable characters or control characters. Since some control characters cannot be processed by a text editor, the programmer must represent these in the form of numeric constants. In order for the assembler to be able to distinguish strings from normal source text, the characters that form a character string are enclosed in delimiters. One delimiter designates the start of the string, and a matching delimiter the end. Typical delimiters are the quotation mark ("), slash (/), and apostrophe (').

Examples: `"Hello ATARI!"`
            `/Hello reader!/`

A special rule concerns the representation of the delimiter itself within a string. To represent the delimiter itself within a string, it must appear as two successive delimiters.

Examples: `"Hello ""reader"""` corresponds to `'Hello "reader"'`
            `/10//5=2/` corresponds to `"10/5=2"`

An arithmetic expression is one or more constants, symbols or functions connected by an operator. Constants and/or symbols of various types occur in a mixed expression. Various operators and functions are available to you depending on the capability of the assembler. These operations are not converted to machine language instructions by the assembler. Rather, these operations are used exclusively for calculating the value of the operands of instructions.

Examples: `10+$0A`
            `LINE+1`
            `NOT 10`

In general, all 68000 assemblers offer all of the basic arithmetic operators and some of the logical operators for generating an expression.

Symbols and system constants

We have talked about using symbols and labels. Now we'll familiarize ourselves with the syntactic rules of symbolic assembly language programming. The assembler must be able to clearly distinguish symbols from the rest of the text in the source file. For this reason there are certain rules regarding the definition of symbols. Generally, symbol names consist of a continuous sequence of letters, digits and certain special characters. Imbedded spaces in a symbol name are not allowed. Symbols must usually be separated from other parts of the source file text by spaces. If the separation can be made clear through other characters, such as with mathematical operators, the spaces can usually be omitted. A symbol may not begin with a digit. This distinguishes between symbols and numbers.

Using a reserved name as a symbol is forbidden. Most assemblers, however, allow a reserved name to appear within a label. Reserved names include all mnemonics, assembler directives, function names, and system constants. System constants are predefined symbol names whose value the assembler itself manages. We'll talk more about the system constants later. Usually the length of a symbol is limited to a maximum number of characters. For obscure reasons, a length of 6 characters is often the maximum for a symbol name. Some assemblers allow arbitrarily long symbol names, but only a certain number of the leading characters are evaluated to distinguish symbols from each other. These are called significant characters. Because of these limitations, the programmer is often forced to find short, easily-remembered abbreviations for his symbols. Some assemblers allow special characters in the symbol name in order to increase our comprehension. Typical special characters allowed are a period (.), underline (_), backslash (\), and colon (:).

Examples: CHROUT

             DATA_IN

             LOOP1:

             SPC.20

System constants are a special group of symbols. The symbol names and the number of system constants are different depending on the assembler. Here are some commonly-used system constants.

Examples: CR   Control character ($0D)

             TRUE, HIGH   True ($FFFF)

             FALSE, LOW   False ($0000)

             *   Current address

The last system constant in our example is not really a constant at all. The value of this symbol is always calculated by the assembler at the start of each program line. The value always remains constant within that line. This symbol always represents the address at which the assembler will place the next machine instruction. Later we'll talk more about this symbol in connection with address calculation.

Mnemonics and mnemonic extensions

In this section we'll take a look at the syntactic rules for the mnemonics or opcodes that determine the actual machine language instructions.

Unfortunately, these mnemonics are not standardized. But there *is* a standard set by the manufacturer and followed by assembler developers. We will make special mention of differences.

As you can easily see on the next pages, a mnemonic is always selected from a specific group of instructions; within it the assembler will find the actual instruction. An instruction group includes only machine language instructions that perform essentially the same function.

We will explain all of the instructions used in this book. The following table serves as an overview and explains principle relationships. You do not have to memorize all of the mnemonics.

```
ABCD.B    OP1,OP2       Add binary-coded decimal, extend
ADD.X     OP1,OP2       Add binary
ADDA.X    OP1,OP2       Add binary to address register
ADDI.X    OP1,OP2       Add immediate
ADDQ.X    OP1,OP2       Add immediate quick
ADDX.X    OP1,OP2       Add binary with extended
AND.X     OP1,OP2       Logical AND
ANDI.X    OP1,OP2       Logical AND with immediate value
ASL.X     OP1(,OP2)     Arithmetic shift left
ASR.X     OP1(,OP2)     Arithmetic shift right
Bcc.X     OP1           Branch if condition code true
BCHG.X    OP1,OP2       Test bit and change
BCLR.X    OP1,OP2       Bit test and clear
BRA.X     OP1           Branch always
BSET.X    OP1,OP2       Bit test and set
BSR.X     OP1           Branch to subroutine
BTST.X    OP1,OP2       Bit test
CHK.W     OP1,OP2       Check register against bounds
CLR.X     OP1           Clear
CMP.X     OP1,OP2       Compare
CMPA.X    OP1,OP2       Compare address register
CMPI.X    OP1,OP2       Compare immediate
CMPM.X    OP1,OP2       Compare in memory
DBcc.X    OP1,OP2       Decrement and branch, conditionally
DIVS.W    OP1,OP2       Divide signed
DIVU.W    OP1,OP2       Divide unsigned
EOR.X     OP1,OP2       Logical exclusive OR
EORI.X    OP1,OP2       Logical exclusive OR with immediate
EXG.L     OP1,OP2       Exchange register
EXT.X     OP1           Sign extend
JMP       OP1           Jump absolute
JSR       OP1           Jump to subroutine absolute
LEA.L     OP1,OP2       Load effective addr to addr register
LINK      OP1,OP2       Link local base pointer
LSL.X     OP1,OP2       Logical shift left
LSR.X     OP1,OP2       Logical shift right
MOVE.X    OP1,OP2       Move source data to destination
MOVEA.X   OP1,OP2       Move to address register
MOVEM.X   OP1,OP2       Move multiple register
MOVEP.X   OP1,OP2       Move from or to peripheral register
MOVEQ.L   OP1,OP2       Move immediate quick
MULS.W    OP1,OP2       Multiply with sign
MULU.W    OP1,OP2       Multiply without sign
```

```
NBCD.B      OP1,OP2         Negate binary-coded decimal
NEG.X       OP1             Negate
NEGX.X      OP1             Negate with extend
NOP                         No operation
NOT.X       OP1             Logical NOT
OR.X        OP1,OP2         Logical OR
ORI.X       OP1,OP2         Logical OR with immediate value
PEA.L       OP1             Push effective address
RESET                       Reset external devices
ROL.X       OP1(,OP2)       Rotate left
ROR.X       OP1(,OP2)       Rotate right
ROXL.X      OP1(,OP2)       Rotate left with extended bit
ROXR.X      OP1(,OP2)       Rotate right with extended bit
RTE                         Return from exception
RTR                         Return and restore register
RTS                         Return from suboutine
SBCD.B      OP1,OP2         Subtract bin. coded dec. with extend
Scc.B       OP1             Set byte according to condition code
STOP        OP1             Stop with condition code loaded
SUB.X       OP1,OP2         Subtract binary
SUBA.X      OP1,OP2         Subtract binary from address reg
SUBI.X      OP1,OP2         Subtract immediate
SUBQ.X      OP1,OP2         Subtract immediate quick
SUBX.X      OP1,OP2         Subtract binary with extend
SWAP.X      OP1             Swap register halves
TAS.B       OP1             Test byte and set always bit 7
TRAP        OP1             Software trap always
TRAPV       OP1             Trap on overflow
TST.X       OP1             Test byte
UNLK        OP1             Unlink local area
```

You probably noticed the .X, .B, .W, and .L extensions on many of the instructions. These mnemonic extensions are used to specify the width of the operand that the instruction will use. The extensions have the following meanings:

.B   operand width BYTE, 8 bits, 1 byte, 1/2 word

.W   operand width WORD, 16 bits, 2 bytes, 1 word

.L   operand width LONG, 32 bits, 4 bytes, 2 words

.X   any of the above operand widths

When you use an instruction in the mnemonic table labelled with .B, .W or .L, it means that this instruction can be used only with this operand width. Some assemblers permit the programmer to omit the extension on these commands. Instructions having .X as the extension can be used with any of the three operand widths. If the extension is omitted when using these commands, the assembler assumes that programmer wants to use the WORD operand width. Commands for which no extension is listed in the mnemonic table have an implicit operand width.

Some instructions in the mnemonic table have a special form of mnemonic extension in the form of two lower-case c's (cc). These are **condition codes**, instructions to test for a specific condition and performing an operation based on the result of the test. The condition code determines the condition that the instruction will test for. The programmer extends the mnemonic with this condition code (cc).

The second column of the table contains the specification of the instruction operands. Some commands have no operands. In this case these instructions specify the operand(s) implicitly. An operand specified in parentheses is optional. We'll explain more about the operand formation later.

Condition codes

We won't examine all of the condition codes of the 68000 flag register. Instead we want to give you a general understanding of the purpose of the condition codes.

68000 instructions that test the flags always refer to one or more of the following flags:

C   carry   carry for addition, borrow for subtraction
N   negative   result is negative (two's complement)
V   overflow   last operation lead to an overflow
Z   zero   result is zero (all bits)

There are two condition codes for each of these flags, depending on whether the programmer is interested in a set (1) or a cleared (0) flag. We'll present these eight condition codes using a conditional branch instruction. The general form of the instruction is Bcc OP1, where OP1 is the branch destination if a test for a specific condition is true (see addressing modes).

C C	BCC OP1	Branch if carry clear	Jump if C = 0
C S	BCS OP1	Branch if carry set	Jump if C = 1
P L	BPL OP1	Branch if plus	Jump if N = 0
M I	BMI OP1	Branch if minus	Jump if N = 1
V C	BVC OP1	Branch if overflow clear	Jump if V = 0
V S	BVS OP1	Branch if overflow set	Jump if V = 1
N E	BNE OP1	Branch if not equal	Jump if Z = 0
EQ	BEQ OP1	Branch if equal	Jump if Z = 1

These condition codes are used when the programmer wants to test the state of the flags. The setting of a flag can take place as a result of a comparison operation. For example, suppose we compare two operands:

```
CMP OP1, OP2
```

As a result of this instruction the **Zero** flag is set or reset. If OP1=OP2, the **Zero** flag is set. If OP1≠OP2 the **Zero** flag is reset. Two condition codes can be used to test the Zero flag: EQ (tests for Zero flag set) and NE (tests for Zero flag reset).

EQ	BEQ OP1	Branch if equal	Jump if OP1 = OP2
NE	BNE OP1	Branch if not equal	Jump if OP1 ≠ OP2

To test for OP1 greater than OP2, OP1 less than OP2 or OP1 equal to OP2, we must recall binary number representation. Binary numbers can be viewed as either signed or unsigned numbers. An example will clarify this:

255 > 0   (%11111111 is greater than %00000000)

-1 < 0   (%11111111 is less than   %00000000)

Note how the numbers are complemented for negative numbers. The 68000 supports the processing of both types of numbers. The following condition codes are used for unsigned numbers:

LO	BLO OP1	Branch lower	Jump if OP2 < OP1
LS	BLS OP1	Branch lower same	Jump if OP2 <= OP1
HI	BHI OP1	Branch higher	Jump if OP2 > OP1
HS	BHS OP1	Branch higher same	Jump if OP2 >= OP1

And for signed numbers:

L T	BLT OP1	Branch less than	Jump if OP2 < OP1
L E	BLE OP1	Branch less/equal	Jumo if OP2 <= OP1
G T	BGT OP1	Branch greater th.	Jump if OP2 > OP1
GE	BGE OP1	Branch greater/eq.	Jump if OP2 >= OP1

It should be noted that these comparison instructions work in conjunction with the CMP instructions. As a result OP1 is always compared to OP2. We will mention two more condition codes having a special relationship to the instructions DBcc.W OP1, OP2 and Scc.B OP1. These are special instructions that affect the execution of the instruction depending on the condition. More on these commands later.

T	ST OP1	TRUE: The condition is always fulfilled
F	DBF, OP1, OP2	FALSE: The condition is never fulfilled

These condition codes have no meaning in connection with the conditional branch instructions. There is another mnemonic for the instruction BT (branch true): BRA (branch always). The variant BF is not allowed since the corresponding opcode would be identical to that of BSR (relative subroutine call)—and it's a little obscure anyway.

Syntax of the addressing modes

By using the addressing modes you can determine what operands an instruction will operate on. In the chapter describing the 68000 microprocessor, we explained the function of all 14 addressing modes.

Here we'll show you how to represent and use the individual addressing modes in assembly language programming. If you take a look at the list of mnemonics, you will see that there are basically four classes of instructions:

- instructions without operands
- instructions with one operand
- instructions with two operands
- instructions with one and optionally two operands

Instructions that do not need an operand represent the first and simplest form of addressing. The instruction contains the addressing mode implicitly. In assembler syntax, implicit addressing is represented by simply writing the mnemonic.

Examples: NOP   no operation
            RESET   reset peripherals
            RTS   return from subroutine

All instructions requiring operands use one or more of the 13 other addressing modes. In theory, any of these addressing modes can be used to generate an opcode. In practice, however, there are some limitations on the combination of instructions and addressing modes in the 68000 instruction set. The instruction overview in the appendix indicates what instructions can be used with a particular addressing mode.

One of the most important addressing modes is **direct register addressing**. A distinction is made between data and address register.

Examples: CLR.L   D0   * clear data register 0

           ADD.L   D1,D0   * D0 = D0 + D1

           ADDA.L   D0,A1   * A1 = A1 + D0

           MOVEA.L A0,A1   * A1 = A0

In the above examples we always used the long-word operand width in order to use all 32 bits. For .W, for instance, only the lower 16 bits are used. In these examples you can also recognize the use of two operands (separated by a comma) and the mixing of two addressing modes (address and data register direct).

If constants are required for an operation, the **immediate addressing mode** is used. In assembler syntax, the immediate operand is written as a "#" (number sign) followed by an arithmetic expression.

Examples: MOVE.L   #30,D0   * D0 = 30 (load D0 with 30)

           ADDI.W   #$A0,D7   * D7 = D7 + 160

           CMPI.B   #CR,D0   * Compare D0 with CR

Many operands' addresses in memory are already known. In these cases the programmer can access this address directly. This access is called **absolute addressing**. The 68000 distinguishes between the addressing modes absolute long and absolute short. When formulating an assembly language program, the programmer does not need to take this difference into consideration, because the assembler itself will chose an appropriate addressing mode based on the size of the operand. In the assembler syntax, we simply specify the desired address as an operand by means of an arithmetic expression.

Examples: MOVE.B $00ABCDEF,D0 * Load byte (abs. long)

            CLR.W $1000   * clear word (short)

Another form of operand addressing is the **address register indirect** mode. Here the absolute address is not given in the instruction, but only an address register that contains the absolute address. In assembler syntax this is indicated by placing the address register in parentheses.

Examples: MOVE.L   D0,(A0)   * D0 to address in A0

            MOVE.B   (A0),(A1)   * Byte from A0 to A1

Note in the last example the transfer of a byte, with address in address register A0, to the address contained in address register A1, without requiring an additional register.

The postincrement and predecrement modes are extensions of the address register indirect addressing mode. As you can see in the last example, tranferring a byte (or any other operand width) is very simple. In practice, however, entire strings of bytes are often processed. Here you must program a loop whereby the address register is incremented by the number of bytes to be transferred. The addressing mode predecrement is the opposite of postincrement. In assembler syntax these addressing modes are represented by prefixed and suffixed addition and subtraction signs.

Examples: CLR.B   (A0)+   * Clear byte and A0=A0+1

            CLR.W   -(A1)   * A1=A1-2 and clear word

            MOVE   (A0)+,(A1)+   * Move word, address+2

            MOVE   (A0)+,(A1)-   * Rotate words: A0 to A1

            MOVE   (A0)+,D0   * Word from A0 to D0, A0+2

Another variant of the address register indirect addressing is the **address register indirect addressing with displacement**. With this addressing mode, a constant value (displacement) is added to the actual address contained in the address register. By using this addressing mode, the programmer can easily access an element of an array without having to change the address register for each access. In assembler syntax, the displacement is specified as an arithmetic expression placed before the indirect addressing.

```
Examples:   CLR.B     0(A0)          * Byte addressed via A0
            CLR.B     1(A0)          * Next byte, A0 unchanged
            MOVE      (A0),1(A0)     * 1st to 2nd byte of A0
```

The addressing mode **indirect address register addressing with displacement and index** (whew!) is an extension of the indirect address register addressing with displacement. In this addressing mode, the contents of the address register, the displacement, and the contents of another data or address register are all added together to form the address of the operand. This addressing mode is also used to access elements of an array with the help of a variable pointer (index). The operand width of the index register (data or address register) can be specified in the instruction. Either a word (.W) or a long word (.L, the entire register) is then used in the addition. To represent this addressing mode in assembler syntax, the index register is placed inside the parentheses after the address register.

```
Examples:   NEG       1(A0,D0.L)     * Negate 2nd word, indexed D0
            NEG       2(A0,A1)       * Neg 3rd word, word index
```

Another form of addressing is the program counter relative mode, or simply **relative addressing**. The relative address involves an index added to the current program counter contents in order to get the effective memory address. This addressing mode is used for conditional jump instructions and for the two special instructions BSR and DBcc. Because relative addressing is defined by the mnemonic used, the programmer need not designate it specially in the instruction. The assembler not only recognizes the addressing mode, it also calculates the relative address of the instruction itself when the programmer specifies the address of the branch destination. We'll talk more about this function of the assembler in connection with address calculation.

```
Examples:  BNE     NOTEQUAL    * Jump on OP1<>OP2
           BSR     CALC        * Relative subroutine jump
           DBF     LOOP        * Jump to the start of the loop
```

A special form of relative addressing is the **program counter relative addressing with displacement** and the **program counter relative addressing index**. These last two addressing modes function identically to the address register indirect addressing with displacement with or without index. These addressing modes are used to write relocatable programs. They cannot be combined with all machine language programs, however. In assembler syntax, these addressing modes are distinguished from the address register indirect addressing by the specification of PC, instead of an address register.

```
Examples:  CLR     ARRAY(PC)     * Clear 1st word in data array
           CLR     ARRAY(PC,A0)  * Clear array, indexed A0
```

In the following sections we'll talk more about the use of these addressing modes. We will also discuss some syntactic details of special instructions.

As you see in the description of the last addressing modes, there are some special reserved names to indicate the special registers of the 68000. In the cause of program counter relative addressing, the **program counter** is indicated by PC. As you have already learned, address register A7 is the user stack pointer, or in the supervisor mode (A7') it's the supervisor stack pointer. To improve the readability of the program, most assemblers allow the use of USP for the user stack pointer and SSP for the supervisor stack pointer. One exception is the use of USP within a MOVE instruction—different instructions will be created with this combination.

Another special register is the **status register** (SR). Part of the status register is the **condition code register** (CCR). The status register can be completely or partially set to a defined value by means of a special MOVE instruction. A read access is possible only on the entire status register. Here again, we refer you to your 68000 microprocessor reference book for more information. Some examples of assembler syntax:

```
Examples:   MOVE      #0,CCR        * Condition code register true
            MOVE      #$1000,USP    * Initialize stack pointer
            MOVE      sr,-(A7)      * Save status on stack
```

In connection with the MOVE instruction, we make mention of a highly specialized operand formation—the **register list**. Some or all of the data and/or address registers can be stored at or loaded from an address simultaneously. The assembler can create the appropriate opcode from the register list. A register list is an enumeration of registers in any order, with the registers separated by slashes ("/"), or a sequence of registers in which the first and last registers are given and connected by a dash ("-").

Examples: MOVEM   D0,-(A7)   * 1 reg on the stack

           MOVEM   D0/A0,-(A7)   * 2 regs on the stack

           MOVEM   (A7)+,D0-D7   * Data regs from stack

           MOVEM   (A7)+,D0-D7/A0-A7 * All regs from the stack

In summary we would like to give you an overview of the syntax rules for the addressing modes, and indicate any deviations in different assemblers.

Addressing Mode	Operand type
Implicit	- - - - - -
Data Register direct	D n
Address Register direct	A n
Immediate	#Data.X
Absolute long	Address.W
Absolute short	Address.L
Address register indirect	(An)
Post increment	(An)+
Predecrement	-(An)
Adr. reg. indirect with displ.	D16(An)
Adr. reg. indirect with displ. and index	D8(An,Rn.X)
Relative	Offset
Relative with displacement	D16(PC)
Relative with displ. and index	D8(PC,Rn.X)
Register list	Di-Dj/Ai-Aj
User stack pointer	USP
Supervisor stack pointer	SSP
Status register	SR
Condition code register	CCR
Program counter	PC

Key:		
	D n	Data registers 0-7
	A n	Address registers 0-7
	R n	Dn or An
	Data	.B, .W, or .L constant
	Address	.W or .L constant
	Offset	.B or .W constant
	D 8	.B constant
	D16	.W constant
	i, j, n	Register number 0-7
	.B	Byte
	.W	Word
	.L	Long word
	.X	.B, .W, or .L
deviations: (seldom)	SP	corresponds to USP
	$	corresponds to PC
	Address	corresponds to address
	Ri, Xi	corresponds to Rn
	D	corresponds to D8 or D16
	A7	corresponds to SSP

Syntax Summary for Addressing Modes

The assembler directives

Every assembler offers a certain number of assembler **directives** (pseudo-opcodes). In general, directives do not create any machine code. For a better overview, we place the most important directives into the following main groups:

- Address calculation, memory management, and organization
- Source text management and pass control
- Tables and data areas
- Symbol declaration
- Macro processing
- Output format and options

Directives are prefixed by a period (".") followed by an abbreviation. The abbreviation or mnemonic can be followed by one or more operands. Generally, the same conditions that apply to the formation of arithmetic expressions apply to the formation of operands.

The most important directive in the first group is the ORG directive. This directive tells the assembler where the generated machine code will run in memory. As a general rule, this is the first instruction in an assembly language program. In any event, the assembler must encounter an ORG directive before the first machine instruction or table can be assembled, so that the assembler can create the appropriate machine code for the defined address.

```
Example:   .ORG    $1000       * Absolute address specification
           .ORG    STARTADDR   * Symbol must be defined
```

Sometimes you may have to reserve space in a program—for instance, to save temporary values. The DS.X pseudo-op is used for this purpose. This directive reserves a specific number of bytes, words, or long words based on the operand width (.X). A corresponding number of fill characters is then generated at the next available address. $00 is usually used as the fill character. At this point it should be mentioned that the programmer can also add a label to a pseudo-op instruction. By doing this, the reserved space can be accessed symbolically.

Examples:

```
          .DS.B  256    * 128 words will be reserved
TAB       .DS.W 128     * 128 words will be reserved
DATA      .DS.L 64      * 128 words will be reserved
BYTE1     .DS.B 1       * 1 byte will be reserved
```

The attentive reader will note a typical problem of defining a table in our last example. As you have already learned, a machine language instruction must always begin on an even address. If the programmer defined a table that comprises an uneven number of bytes, the next machine instruction would begin on odd address. To avoid this, the EVEN directive is used to advance the address counter of the assembler to the next even address. There are also some assemblers that automatically preserve the word alignment after defining tables.

Example:

```
DATA      .DS.B 3          * Reserve 3 bytes
          .EVEN            * Align to word boundary
START     MOVE.B D0,DATA   * Fill table
```

We said that the area reserved by the DS directive is filled with $00. But there are also assemblers that permit you to fill the area with an alternate character. The FILL directive is used to define an alternate fill character.

Examples: .FILL $20   * Fill with spaces
            .FILL "A"   * Fill with A ($41)

Another form of the DS.X directive is the DC.X directive. With this directive, a memory area can be reserved and also filled with constants (table). The programmer can give a list of alphanumeric expressions, separated by commas, following the directive that are then placed in memory.

Examples: TAB   .DC.B 1,"A" * Creates $0141
                   .DC.W 1,"A" * Creates $0001,$4100
                   .DC.L 1   * Creates $0000,$0001
                   .DC.L "AB"   * Creates $4142,$0000

In the above examples, note the special treatment of strings. Strings are filled with $00 to the full length of the operand. As a general rule, the address counter of the assembler is not automatically advanced to the next even address after a DC.X directive (EVEN directive), so that several DC's can form a contiguous table. Some assemblers automatically recognize the end of multiple DC.X directives and correct the address counter to an even address as soon as an instruction following a DC.X is not DC.X.

Another important task of an assembler is the definition of symbols and labels that cannot be assigned a value by the assembler (external jumps, constants). These definitions are made by the EQU psuedo-op. No distinction is made as to whether the name is a symbol (data) or a label (address). A symbol can be assigned any value, as represented by an arithmetic expression, up to a maximum of 32 bits. A symbol may be defined only once. If a symbol must be assigned a new value, some assemblers offer a REDEF directive. Some examples clarify the assembler syntax of these directives:

```
Examples:  ADDRESS .EQU   $1234    * corresponds to $00001234
           CHAR    .EQU   "A"      * corresponds to $00000001
           TEXT    .EQU   "ABC"    * corresponds to $00414243


           TEXT    .REDEF CR       * corresponds to $00000000
```

Another group of directives allows the inclusion of multiple source files (separately created) that can be combined into a single machine language program. Multiple source files may be chained together with the FILE psuedo-op. The directive specifies the next source file which is to be assembled as part of the machine language program. The INCLUDE psuedo-op is similar; it's used to insert a source file at that particular point in the current source file.

Example:

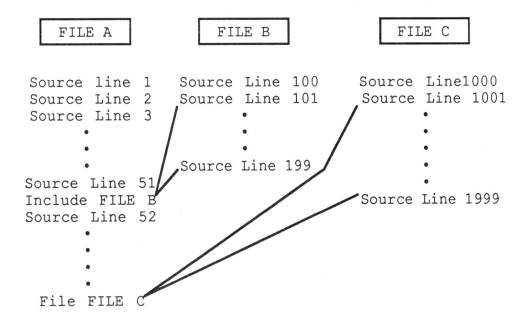

The programmer has other directives available to alter the order of assembly. The simplest directive is .END. This directive indicates that the end of the source has been reached.

Example: .END   * End assembly

Conditional assembly is controlled by a another group of directives. Here a condition is tested before a designated portion of the source text is assembled, and the assembly of this source text is performed only if the condition is true. If the condition is not true, this portion of the source text is excluded from the assembly.

Before we go into the syntax rules for these directives, we would like to illustrate the use of conditional assembly.

Let's assume that you are developing a program that will be used in both English and German. You could first develop the program in English and then make a German translation when the development is complete. You might discover that it isn't possible to make a direct translation of the English words. Often an entire screen needs to be changed because a single word has become too long and no logical abbreviation or replacement can be found. Such modifications often require a large number of subsequent changes. When the program is finished, even an experienced programmer might find it too difficult to coordinate the changes.

One alternative is conditional assembly. If you're writing a segment of a program and anticipate changes will be required for the German version, you can then program both versions of the segment and test them. By means of conditional assembly you can specify only the English or German portion be assembled with the neutral language-dependent portions. In conditional assembly, an arithmetic expression is evaluated and the result examined. If the result is true (not zero), the condition is satisfied; if the result is zero, the condition is not satisfied. In our example, the programmer could define a symbol "LANGUAGE" as 0 for English and 1 for German, and use this symbol for the conditional assembly. A portion of the source file to be conditionally assembled is introduced by the following directives:

```
Examples:   .IFE   LANGUAGE     * Assemble if LANGUAGE=0
            .IFN   LANGUAGE     * Assemble if LANGUAGE<>0
```

The source file to be conditionally assembled is followed with the ENDIF directive. If the condition was unsatisfied, the assembly continues at this line.

Example: .ENDIF   * End of conditional assembly

Some assembler allow limited interaction with the programmer during assembly. Two directives are used for this. The PRINT directive allows outputting of messages to the screen. The programmer can make a keyboard input by means of the INPUT directive. The assembler then assigns the keyboard input to a symbol, similar to the EQU directive. The INPUT directive is especially useful in the development and test phase of a program, when there are much-used variable parameters to change. This form of programming allows you to avoid using the editor just to change a few parameters. In reference to our previous example (English/German), you could output a question regarding the language and assign a control value (0 or 1) to the symbol LANGUAGE by means of keyboard input. The following example should clarify the assembler syntax:

Example: .PRINT   "English (0) or German (1)?",CR
            .INPUT LANGUAGE

Another group of directives handles the format control. These directives can control the format of the assembler listing. Moreover, the programmer can use certain options to adapt the list to his/her needs, or make it easier to read (program documentation). The following list illustrates the many possibilities and explains the syntax rules:

Examples: .NOLIST   * Do not create a listing

.LIST   * Create listing again

.PAGE   * Move to a new page

.NOFORMAT   * No formatted output

.FORMAT   * Output listing formatted

.SPC   3   * Print three blank lines

.LLEN   80   * Format 80 characters/line

.LINE   72   * Set page length to 72 lines

.TOP   6   * 6 blank lines between pages

.TITLE   "Text" * Define page title

.XPUNCH   * No hex dump creation

.PUNCH   * Create hex dump again

.NOCROSSREF   * Suppress cross reference

.CROSSREF   * Print cross reference

Some assemblers manage the assembly control options by means of an OPTION directive. Here each assembly control option does not have its own directive, but shares a common directive with all control options. The option list behind the OPTION directive controls which controls are on or off.

Examples: .OPTION NOLIST, NOPUNCH, NOFORMAT
           .OPTION LIST, PUNCH, FORMAT

Assembler directives are generally the least standardized elements of assembly language programming. We have tried to give you a look at the possible range and uses of directives. You can learn the syntax rules of your own assembler by reading your assembler manual.

Macro processing with an assembler

We have already explained the possibilities that macro processing offers. Here we would like to familiarize you with the syntax rules. The macro definition and macro call are created with assembler instructions similar to directives.

```
Example:  .MACRO      BYTEARRAY_ADR(XIND,YIND,ADDR)
          MOVEM   D0,-(SP)           * Save register
          MOVE.W  YIND,D0            * Y-index for multiplication
          MULU.W  #100,D0            * *BYTES per line
          ADD.L   XIND,D0            * Add X-index
          ADDI.L  #BASE,D0           * +Table start address
          MOVE.L  D0,ADDR            * Save address
          MOVEM   (SP)+,D0           * Register to old value
          .ENDM                      * End of definition

          ...BYTEARRAY_ADR (XPNT,YPNT,ST)
```

In our example, the address of a byte within a two-dimensional table is calculated. It should be noted that a macro does not involve a subroutine call, but the assembler behaves as if the source text of the macro definition had been written at the place where the macro call occurred. Macros are written when a given sequence of instructions are used several times in a program.

Here the assembler must know the type of data (symbols or labels) the macro will use. The programmer tells the assembler in the macro definition what symbols within the macro definition should be replaced by other symbols in the macro call. All symbols within the macro definition have validity only within the macro, in order to avoid multiple definition problems in multiple macro calls. However, the programmer can use any external symbol inside the macro.

To further clarify the function of macro processing, we'll show you what the assembler does when a macro is called twice.

```
...BYTEARRAY_ADR  (XINDEX,YINDEX,ADDRESS)
```

```
MOVEM    D0,-(SP)       * Save register
MOVE.W   YINDEX,D0      * Y-index for multiplication
MULU.W   #100,D0        * *Bytes per line
ADD.L    XINDEX,D0      * Add X-index
ADDI.L   #BASE,D0       * +Table start address
MOVE.L   D0,ADDRESS     * Save address
MOVEM    (SP)+,D0       * Register to old value
```

```
...BYTEARRAY_ADR  (XPNT,YPNT,ST)
```

```
MOVEM    D0,-(SP)       * Save register
MOVE.W   YPNT,D0        * Y-index for multiplication
MULU.W   #100,D0        * *Bytes per line
ADD.L    XPNT,D0        * Add X-index
ADDI.L   #BASE,D0       * +Table start address
MOVE.L   D0,ST          * Save address
MOVEM    (SP)+,D0       * Register to old value
```

Address calculation

To extend your understanding of assembly language programming and the operation of the assembler, let's turn to the topic of address calculation. Address calculation, next to the translation of mnemonics, is the most important task of the assembler. From another angle, many typical "beginner's" mistakes have to do with address calculation.

Most assemblers allow a source file to be written completely symbolically. In the most extreme case, the program defines all constants and external addresses as symbols and labels (declarations). These symbols don't give the assembler any trouble, because their values are pre-defined. The labels defined within a program, destinations for branches, subroutine calls, and accesses to tables, are more difficult for the assembler to process. To understand these difficulties, think back to the assembly operation.

The text of a source file is processed by the assembler line by line, starting with the first line. If a symbol definition occurs within a line, the symbol is entered into a table together with its corresponding value. This symbol table contains all of the symbols (and their values) defined up to this point. If a symbol is used as an operand during the assembly, the assembler searches for the symbol in the symbol table and replaces it by the value from the symbol table. The assembler may have difficulty in discerning between symbols contained in the table already and those defined in a later line.

If the symbol is contained in the table, then it was definitely defined in a previous line. This case is called a backward reference. If the symbol is not in the table, it may be defined later in the program. This is called a forward reference.

These forward references form the basic problem of address calculation. In order to translate an instruction, the assembler also needs the value of a forward reference. The assembler uses a simple trick to overcome these difficulties. It makes two passes through the text of the source file. In the first pass, no machine code is generated. At the end of the first pass, all symbols and values found are contained in the symbol table. If this is not the case, an error message is issued with the assembly containing errors. This is why a symbolic assembler is also called a two-pass assembler.

Yet the programmer can still easily "confuse" the assembler even though the source code is syntactically and logically correct. Many assemblers become "trapped" by these constructions; we want to familiarize you with some of these errors.

The first are the programmer errors of "cyclical definitions."

```
Example:   SYMBOL1    .EQU  SYMBOL2    * First definition
           SYMBOL2    .EQU  SYMBOL3    * Second definition
           SYMBOL3    .EQU  SYMBOL1    * Third definition
```

It is easy to see why this leads to an error because, in the final analysis, none of the symbols are defined. It behaves differently in the following case, which is very similar to the above.

```
Example:   SYMBOL1    .EQU  SYMBOL2    * First definition
           SYMBOL2    .EQU  SYMBOL3    * Second definition
           SYMBOL3    .EQU  1234567    * Value is known
```

In this example we have a multiple forward reference. It is easy to see why a simple two-pass assembler would have trouble with it if we try to the assembly once "by hand." After pass 1, SYMBOL1 and SYMBOL2 are undefined. In pass 2, SYMBOL1 cannot be defined because SYMBOL2 is still not defined. SYMBOL2 can be defined in pass 2, since SYMBOL3 is known in pass 1. But already in pass 2 an error is generated in the definition of SYMBOL1 (Whoa!).

Another source of errors is a phase error, although most assemblers can no longer be "tripped up" by them. They are a deviation between the address calculation in pass 1 and the address calculation in pass 2, which the assembler usually recognizes and corrects. These phase errors are created by machine language instructions that have a variable instruction length depending on the size of the operand. If the operand is defined by a forward reference in such an instruction, the assembler reserves the maximum length for the instruction in pass 1 and calculates the symbolic address accordingly. If the instruction becomes shorter in pass 2 as the result of a smaller operand than was assumed in pass 1, all references to following labels must be corrected corresponding to this reduction.

The assembler listing

We have already talked about the assembler listing and format options. Here we'll go into some of the details and characteristics of error handling.

On the next page you see a typical assembler listing. In the list that follows, we do not go into the content of the example program, but we'll explain the individual elements of the listing.

157

①

```
C P / M   6 8 0 0 0   A s s e m b l e r          Revision 04.03        Page   1
Source File: B:DEMO.S
```

②

```
 1
 2  ④
 3                       **************************************      ⑪
 4                       *** FLASH SCREEN    DEMO LISTING ***
 5                       **************************************          ⑩
 6   ⑤      ⑥                           ⑧    ⑨
 7 00000000 7E09                      move.l  #9,d7          * number of flashes
 8                          ⑦
 9 00000002 2C7C00078000    flash:  movea.l  #$78000,a6     * pointer to screen
10
11 00000008 469E            loop:   not.L   (a6)+           * invert
12
13 0000000A BDFC000F8000            cmpa.l  #$78000+$80000,a6 * screen end?
14 00000010 65F6                    blo     loop            * No: continue
15
16 00000012 2C3C0004FFFF            move.l  #$4ffff,d6      * delay loop
17
18 00000018 5386            delay:  subq.l  #1,d6           * until d6=0
19
20 0000001A 0C8600000000            cmpi.l  #0,d6           * test
21 00000020 66F6                    bne     delay           * No: wait
22
23 00000022 51CFFFDE                dbf.w   d7,flash        * repeat if necessary
24
25 00000026 3F3C0000                move.w  #0,-(sp)        * Code: WARMSTART
26 0000002A 4E41                    trap    #1              * call GEMDOS
27
28
29 0000002C                         .end
```

```
C P / M   6 8 0 0 0   A s s e m b l e r          Revision 04.03        Page   2
Source File: B:DEMO.S
```

```
S y m b o l   T a b l e   ⑫
```

```
delay    00000018 TEXT  flash    00000002 TEXT  loop     00000008 TEXT
```

⑬

1) **Title**, changeable by the programmer

2) **Filename** of the source text being processed

3) **Page numbering**, running numbering

4) **Source text line number**, running numbering

5) **Memory address** of the instruction or table

6) **HEX dump** of the instruction or table

7) **Label field**, contains the label name of the line

8) **Mnemonic field**, contains mnemonics or directives

9) **Operand field**, contains operands/addressing mode

10) **Comment field**, contains comments

11) **Comment line**, comment occupies entire line

12) **Symbol table**, listing of all the symbols

13) **Symbol value** (addresses, data) of the symbols

The assembler error analysis distinguishes between simple errors, fatal errors, and warnings. The last indicate possible sources of error, without leading to an interruption of the assembly, because the programmer may explicitly want the indicated situation under certain circumstances. As examples, the assembler points out unreferenced symbols, or indicate that a smaller operand width could be used for an instruction.

Fatal errors are errors that interrupt the assembly because it no longer makes sense to continue. A missing symbol declaration is a fatal error.

Some assemblers handle normal errors, such as a branch over too long a distance, as fatal errors. In spite of the danger of subsequent errors, it may make sense to continue the assembly up to the first fatal error, and simply display the errors found. This method has the advantage that many simple errors (such as syntax errors) can be recognized in the first assembly. The programmer can then correct more than just one error at a time. This saves a great deal of time during development.

The error handling and the layout of the assembler listing differ widely from assembler to assembler, so we must refer you to your assembler documentation again. There you will find a description of all the error messages and warnings.

Using the assembler

Suppose you have edited a source file and now want to translate it into machine language using the assembler. We assume that you have created the source file with an editor, that you have saved the source text on diskette, and have exited the editor program. At this point you will find yourself on the command level of the assembler package. Usually this command level is the TOS or GEM mode—at the operating system level. The assembler can be started from this level.

Before the assembler can start with the conversion, it requires the filename of the source text to be assembled. The assembler may ask you for the name after it is called, or it may be that the programmer simply passes the filename, together with the program name of the assembler, at the command level (operating system). The TOS operating system passes the filename as a parameter to the assembler.

Examples: `A:ASSEM` ....Call
           `File?` `TEXT.SRC` ....Read parameter

           `A:ASSEM TEST.SRC` ....Call with parameter

In addition to the filename, the programmer can specify assembler options at the assembler call. These are control functions for the object code file and the assembler listing. By means of these control parameters the programmer can suppress generation of the object code or direct the output of the listing to a printer or the screen.

Examples: `A:ASSEM` ....Call
           `File?` `TEST.SRC` ....Source text
           `Object?` `ABS.OBJ` ....Object file name
           `Listing?` `P` ....Output to printer

           `A:ASSEM TEST.SRC/ABS.OBJ/P` ....Parameters

With some assemblers control parameters must be entered. If they are missing, the assembler uses default values. The specific defaults your assembler uses and how the assembler is called are explained in your manual.

The debugger

We have already mentioned the debugger/monitor. Here we'll give you an overview of the use of these programming aids and their capabiltites.

As a general rule, the debugger is initiated much like the assembler. The name of the machine language program to be tested is usually entered as a parameter.

Examples: `DDT`   ....Call the debugger
           `DDT TEST.OBJ`   ....Call and load TEST

The Atari ST's debugger is designated SID (Symbolic Instruction Debugger). The SID is an improvement over earlier debuggers in thay it allows symbolic processing of a program. In this section we'll explain the basic operation of this tool.

The tasks of a debugger/monitor program can be broken up into four basic groups:

- Read/write program (memory area) from/to disk
- Display and/or change memory/register contents
- Test the program (trace and breakpoint)
- Aid functions (hex/dec conversion, arithmetic, etc.)

After initiating the debugger, you are at the command level. This means that the debugger waits for you to enter a command, which must be followed with the <RETURN> key. Keep in mind that the debugger is usually a rather primitive and unintelligent tool. The command structure is extremely rigid and very sensitive to input errors. Syntactic and logical errors are acknowleged with very terse messages. The programmer should also be very familiar with programming at the machine level, since changes in the address space can cause the computer to crash.

In this section we won't go into each individual command of the debugger. Instead, we'll present some interesting details that will introduce you to the test phase. In the end, the debugger is the only tool with which a programmer can track down a program error.

The debugger that you use may have a slightly different command structure. In any event, you should use the documentation included with your debugger. The following list illustrates the commands found in a typical debugger (SID with the Atari Development System).

Ename	Load a program for testing
V	Display parameters of the loaded program
Iname	Generate file control block (FCB) (from the name)
Rname	Load a memory area from disk
Wname,s,f	Write memory area from s to f address
Ds	Hex/ASCII display of bytes at address s
Ds,f	Hex/ASCII display of bytes from address s to f
DWs	Hex/ASCII display of words at address s
DLs	Hex/ASCII display of long words at address s
Ls	Disassemble at address s
Ls,f	Disassemble from address s to address f
X	Display the 68000 registers, Rn, PC, USP, SSP,ST
Xr	Change a register (r=Rn,PC,USP,SSP,ST)
Ss b...b	Write bytes (b) at address s in memory
SWs w...w	Write words (w) at address s in memory
SLs 1...1	Write long word (l) at address s in memory
Fs,f,x	Fill memory from s to f with byte (b)
FWs,f,x	Fill memory from s to f with word (w)
FLs,f,x	Fill memory from s to f with long word (l)
Ms,f,d	Copy memory from s to f to d (b)
G	Start program at current PC
Gs	Start program at address s
Gs,b1...b2	Start program at address s with breakpoints
T	Trace program at current PC
Tn	Trace n machine language instructions at PC
U	Execute 1 machine instruction at PC
Un	Execute program, trace n instructions
K	Displays symbol table information
Hx1,x2	Generate sum and difference of x1 and x2

Key:

name	= filename	s	= start address	f	= end address
r	= register	b	= byte	w	= word
l	= long word	x	= b/w/l	d	= destination addr
bn	= breakpoint	n	= number (1..n) ...		= sequence

One of the most useful functions of the debugger is **disassembly**. This is the exact opposite of assembly. The disassembled program is displayed on the screen not only as a hex dump, but in assembler notation. The display includes mnemonics, operands and addressing modes. This form of representation is very easy to read and makes it easier to find errors.

The **trace** function is probably the debugger's most important test aid. It allows a machine language program to be executed in the single-step mode, one instruction at a time. The program being tested can be so processed, except for certain limitations involving the operating system routines and particularly time-critical program segments (interrupts). In the single-step mode, the current register-set contents are displayed after each instruction.

Breakpoints are another extension of the trace mode. Here the program under test is not processed step-by-step. However, the programmer has the option of interrupting the program at a given address (breakpoint). The debugger watches the machine language program and interrupts execution when the processor comes to the address of a breakpoint. At this point the current register contents of the processor are displayed. In addition to the other manipulation commands of the debugger, you can check the output of your program up to the breakpoint.

Procedure conventions

As a general rule, machine language programs will run on a computer without any additional help; the operating system supports the essential functions of a computer. You will not have to program all of the functions yourself in machine language programming. Instead, you can use operating system routines (to output a character on the screen, for example) without having to consider the hardware-dependent aspects of these functions.

These operating system functions are standardized. Therefore, programs that access operating system routines can run on any computer using the same microprocessor and operating system. One or more parameters are passed to the function when using an operating system function. After execution of the function, a result is passed back to the calling program. Procedure conventions refer to how parameters are passed, how the function is called, and where the result will be expected.

Another form of procedure convention relates to the machine language program. The object program must be provided with a specific identification code and information about the executable program (start address, program length, etc.), so that it can be executed from the operating system.

The procedure conventions are rigidly specified as far as the operating system is concerned. We urge you adhere to certain procedure conventions, and also to the modularization of your own machine language programs.

The simplest form is passing parameters through registers. Here all parameters are passed in the data and/or address registers. The results are also returned in certain registers. As a general rule, unused registers are not changed. If additional registers are required by a function, they are saved at the start of the function and restored again at the end. The registers are usually saved on the stack.

In our examples we'll usually pass parameters in registers. When other forms are used (programming recursion, etc.), we'll point them out.

Another form of parameters passing is the definition of specific memory ranges for passing values. After execution of the function, the results are made available at a defined location in the parameter block. A parameter block can reside at a predetermined address in memory. As a general rule, the programmer passes the start of the parameter block to the function in an address register.

The most elegant way of passing parameters is by the user stack, or self-defined stacks using the address registers. This method is also supported by the 68000 instructions LINK and UNLINK. This parameter passing is similar to the parameter block. However, the parameter area is not stored at a set address in memory, but it is dynamically managed on the stack. We'll use this form of parameter passing when talking about recursive programming.

When using procedures and operating system routines, input and output parameters are defined by procedure conventions. Distinctions are made between the following types of calls:

167

- Subroutine call with start address of the routine

- Subroutine call via a jump table. Here a complete sequence of branch instructions are defined in memory one after the other. The individual branch instructions branch to the actual routines that perform the function. The programmer uses only the address of the branch instruction in the jump table when calling the subroutine.

- Subroutine call of a defined routine in which the function is passed by means of a function number. The actual function is called by means of the function number in the called routine.

- Function call via traps. A function number is usually passed. The actual routine that performs the functions is defined in the vector table of the 68000. The operating system in the Atari ST uses this form of function call extensively.

Merging assembly language routines with high-level languages

When programming in a high-level language, often problems are encountered that can only be solved with an assembly language routine, or can be performed much faster in assembly language. For example, many compilers generate code for graphics programs—a slow process. To accelerate such programs, we might write routines in assembly language that accomplish the same graphics, but are considerably faster.

But now we encounter the problem of combining the assembly language module with the high-level language program. Even with "classically" interpreted languages like BASIC, we can write time-critical segments of the program in assembly language.

To do so, we must follow the procedure conventions of the high-level language exactly (however painful) in the assembly language programs. Here are some important guidelines for doing this.

- are the parameters passed correctly?
- is the result returned properly?
- is the stack changed?
- are the registers used (to the degree required by the convention) saved and reloaded?
- does the stack ever grow beyond a set boundary in the program?
- are data moved to illegal areas?
- will the assembly language program be interrupted by interrupts?
- will the memory area processed by the assembly language program be changed by a DMA operation?

A linker is used to merge assembly language routines with high-level language compiled programs. The assembly language routine is then called by name in the high-level language program. The linker ensures that the addresses in the assembly language program are known by the high-level language program.

In BASIC programs, the assembly language routine is usually called by the command "CALL address" (or SYS..., USR...). The user must ensure that the machine language routine is loaded at the correct address.

Chapter Seven

Programming Step by Step

- •Introduction
- •Example "Decimal/binary conversion"

Introduction

This chapter will introduce you to practical assembly language programming, step by step. At this point we assume you know the material in Chapter 3 and Chapter 6 of this book. If you do not understand the layout of the 68000 microprocessor, or the use of your assembler, we suggest you turn to Chapter 3 and Chapter 6 first.

Our example is intended to show you the step-by-step development of a short decimal to binary conversion routine. We have taken care to avoid any "tricks" concerning existing operating system functions. On one hand, we would like to slowly introduce you to the capabilities of the 68000; on the other hand, we don't want to "spoil" you with all of the comforts of the operating system. In this way we hope that what you learn here will be easily applied to other computer systems.

Decimal/binary conversion

Problem description

Here's our problem: convert a decimal number to a binary number in a machine language program. As you know, a decimal number is equal to its binary equivalent in value; only the representation (number base) is different.

First let's clarify what data the program will work with. In our example the decimal number is the input, and the binary number is the output. For the time being let's just group the individual steps of the conversion under the heading "conversion." Now that we have all of the information, we can draw a data flow plan.

Data flow plan

On this page you see the data flow plan of our example program. The data flow shows the *path* and *type* of data. It shows *what* and *when* something happens with the data. Because of the simplicity of our example, we make no futher comment.

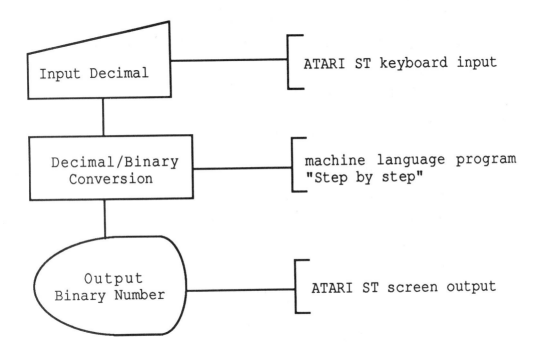

Flowchart

By using the flowchart, we can clarify how the data is processed. You can refine the problem step by step until an exact description of all the instructions for the processor is finally created. The process is called Top-Down programming; the flowchart should illustrate this method.

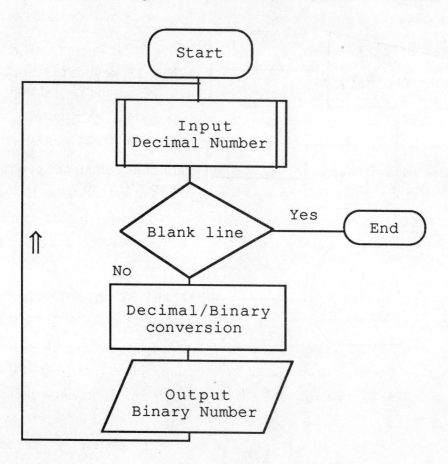

The first step: character output

We turn now to the first step of formulating the algorithm. We want to represent an ASCII character on the screen. The screen doesn't recognize any letters or characters as we recognize them. The picture we see on the monitor is an exact copy of a 32K memory area in the Atari ST. Each bit in the memory is assigned to a point on the screen. A set bit appears dark and a cleared bit is illuminated (on a monochrome monitor).

There is a table in the operating system that determines, bit-by-bit, the appearance of all of the printable characters (the character generator). You can imagine the work involved when outputting an ASCII character. The address of a character in the character generator is calculated, the address of the character pattern onscreen is determined, and the character is copied from the character generator to the screen. Alternatively, the operating system may have to perform special functions for special control characters.

A programmer would have a lot of work to do if the operating system did not perform these elementary functions. As we have already explained, the ST's operating system is a large, complex program. After the operating system is loaded and has started a program, the loaded program takes responsibility for all subsequent actions. The machine language programmer is faced with the problem of how to pass control back and forth between the program and the operating system, to accomplish certain tasks (such as character input and output) using the operating system routines. The authors of the operating system specify these conventions, or individual operating system routines.

```
C P / M   6 8 0 0 0   A s s e m b l e r              Revision 04.03        Page  1
Source File: B:STEP1.S

  1
  2
  3                                 ***********************************************
  4                                 ** Output of an ASCII character      step 1 **
  5                                 ***********************************************
  6
  7
  8 00000000 3F3C0041               move.w  #65,-(sp)           * output "A"
  9 00000004 3F3C0002               move.w  #2,-(sp)            * Code: CONOUT
 10 0000000B 4E41                   trap    #1                  * call GEMDOS
 11 0000000A 588F                   addq.l  #4,sp               * stack correction
 12
 13 0000000C 3F3C000D               move.w  #13,-(sp)           * output CR
 14 00000010 3F3C0002               move.w  #2,-(sp)            * Code: CONOUT
 15 00000014 4E41                   trap    #1                  * call GEMDOS
 16 00000016 588F                   addq.l  #4,sp               * stack correction
 17
 18 00000018 3F3C000A               move.w  #10,-(sp)           * output LF
 19 0000001C 3F3C0002               move.w  #2,-(sp)            * Code: CONOUT
 20 00000020 4E41                   trap    #1                  * call GEMDOS
 21 00000022 588F                   addq.l  #4,sp               * stack correction
 22
 23 00000024 3F3C0000               move.w  #0,-(sp)            * Code: WARMSTART
 24 00000028 4E41                   trap    #1                  * call GEMDOS
 25
 26 0000002A                        .end
```

Here's our first short machine language program. It demonstrates outputting an ASCII character on the screen using an operating system routine. Basically, we are using the GEM-DOS interface of the ST. Complete compatibility with later releases of the ST is guaranteed only by using the GEM-DOS interface.

In our example, no starting address is defined in the assembly language program. Later, the linker is used to combine several assembled programs into one file. Then, the relocating modifier program creates a program to run in any memory space prior to execution. In any case, the programs we present in this book are directly executable under GEM or TOS.

Lines 8-10 output a character (ASCII character A) to the screen. The screen position of the output is always the current cursor position. After outputting the character (or control character), the new cursor position is calculated by the operating system and saved for the subsequent output.

Let's take a close look at how the operating system is used. Basically, one or more parameters are passed to GEM-DOS. These parameters are passed via the stack. Let's follow what happens here. The first parameter passed is the character to be printed (line 8). The operand width is one word. As you know, the ASCII code contains a maximum of 256 characters. For the ST, each different character requires one byte. Parameter passing via the stack is always done in words, since the stack data always begins with an even byte address. The upper half of the ASCII word has no function. But in order to maintain compatibility with possible new character sets (which may exceed 256 characters), we recommend that you ignore the high-order half and keep it filled with binary zeros.

A second parameter is placed on the stack in line 9. This is a **function number**—it tells the operating system what it should do with the data on the stack. The number of parameters is also stated implicitly by the function code. The collection of parameters and function numbers is called a **parameter block**. Our example's parameter block consists of two words (one representing the character, and one the GEM-DOS function code).

The operating system (GEM-DOS) is called by the TRAP instruction in line 10. We aren't really interested in all of the details of this call. However, the sketch below clarifies exactly what must happen in the preparation of the operating system call. Note that, internally, the operating system always works with the supervisor stack. The 68000 is placed into the supervisor mode after a TRAP, an exception. It gets data from the stack that was active when the function is called. This usually involves the user stack, because user programs are executed in the user mode.

You must ensure that all parameters are removed from the stack again after calling an operating system routine. This is done in our example by the ADDQ.L instruction to the stack pointer.

The TRAP instruction works here like a subroutine call. The address of this subroutine is defined by the TRAP number. The processor finds the address of the operating system routine to be called by the TRAP instruction in the vector table of the 68000 system. Once the operating system routine has been executed, the machine language program continues with the next instruction (line 13).

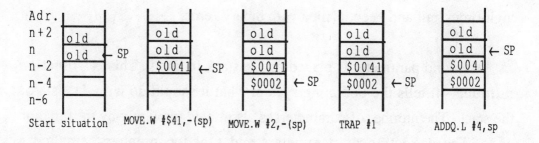

Lines 13 thru 21 repeat the function just described, but here we do not output a printable character. These are the control characters carriage return (CR) and linefeed (LF). A carriage return causes the cursor to be set to the start of the current line. A linefeed moves the cursor down one line. The cursor remains in the same column. If the cursor is already in the last line, the screen is "scrolled." This means that all of the screen lines are moved up one line. The top line disappears from the screen and a blank line is inserted at the lowest line position. In effect, the screen behaves like a sheet of paper in a typewriter.

The instructions in lines 23 and 24 of our example return control to the operating system. This operating system call requires no additional parameters besides the function number.

With this short example we have already told you three basic things about machine language programming. We have explained the principle of operating system calls, outputting characters, and returning to the operating system. To solve our example problem we must still explain how characters are passed from keyboard to the program (character input) through the operating system.(By the way, this method of problem-solving is called Bottom-Up programming, as opposed to the Top-Down method mentioned earlier). Let's take a look at another example program, on the following page.

```
 1
 2
 3                                    ***************************************************
 4                                    **  Input of an ASCII character      step 2 **
 5                                    ***************************************************
 6
 7
 8 00000000 3F3C0001                  move.w  #1,-(sp)        * Code: CONIN
 9 00000004 4E41                      trap    #1              * call GEMDOS
10 00000006 548F                      addq.l  #2,sp           * stack correction
11
12 00000008 3E00                      move.w  d0,d7           * save character
13
14 0000000A 3F3C000D                  move.w  #13,-(sp)       * output CR
15 0000000E 3F3C0002                  move.w  #2,-(sp)        * Code: CONOUT
16 00000012 4E41                      trap    #1              * call GEMDOS
17 00000014 588F                      addq.l  #4,sp           * stack correction
18
19 00000016 3F3C000A                  move.w  #10,-(sp)       * output LF
20 0000001A 3F3C0002                  move.w  #2,-(sp)        * Code: CONOUT
21 0000001E 4E41                      trap    #1              * call GEMDOS
22 00000020 588F                      addq.l  #4,sp           * stack correction
23
24 00000022 CE7C00FF                  and.w   #$ff,d7         * mask character
25
26 00000026 3F07                      move.w  d7,-(sp)        * output character
27 00000028 3F3C0002                  move.w  #2,-(sp)        * Code: CONOUT
28 0000002C 4E41                      trap    #1              * call GEMDOS
29 0000002E 588F                      addq.l  #4,sp           * stack correction
30
31 00000030 3F3C0000                  move.w  #0,-(sp)        * Code: WARMSTART
32 00000034 4E41                      trap    #1              * call GEMDOS
33
34 00000036                           .end
```

The second step: character input

In STEP 2 on the previous page, we demonstrate inputting a character from the keyboard. As a check to see if the routine really works, we echo—that is, immediately output the character to the screen.

Lines 8-9 call the operating system function CONIN (function code 1). This function has no additional parameters. After the routine is called, the operating system waits until a key is pressed on the keyboard. If a key is pressed, the ASCII code is determined and passed to the calling program in the D0 register. For further processing we correct the stack (line 10) and copy the contents of the D0 register to the D7 register with the MOVE instruction (line 12). Lines 14 to 22 you recognize from our first example. These lines reposition the cursor to the first column of the next line.

When calling the character output routine, the contents of the D0 register are changed. Therefore we created a copy of the character entered in the D7 register in line 12. Before we echo the character again, we make sure that the high-order byte is set to zero. Here we use the AND operation (in line 24). In this logical function, all the bits of the constant $FF are combined with the corresponding bits of the D7 register.

Example of AND Instruction

31	30	29	. . .	9	8	7	6	5	4	3	2	1	0	BIT
0	0	0	. . .	0	0	1	1	1	1	1	1	1	1	CONSTANT
x	x	x	. . .	x	x	A	A	A	A	A	A	A	A	CHARACTER
0	0	0	. . .	0	0	A	A	A	A	A	A	A	A	RESULT

183

The above illustration clearly shows what happens in an AND operation. The bit positions containing a zero in the constant always yield a zero in the corresponding RESULT bit position. The bit positions containing a one in the CONSTANT *and* original CHARACTER always yield a one in the corresponding RESULT bit positions. The use of the AND instruction is sometimes called **masking**.

At this point we would also like to clarify the conventions we have used in our examples. In our examples we'll define only one simple register convention. All parameters are passed via address or data registers. The registers are used in descending order according to their first use (D7, D6, D5, ... D3 and A5) They are saved and restored again after use. This eliminates any conflict in register use among subroutines. We would like to point out that this a very simple convention that may not be appropriate for more complex programs.

Back to our second example. The masked character is printed on the screen by calling the operating system routine CONOUT (console output) in lines 26-29. Lines 31 and 32 end the program as before.

With our two examples we already have the important information about the operating system that we need to convert decimal numbers to binary. We won't concern ourselves with additional operating system routines in this chapter.

Our next example brings us one step closer to the problem solution. We want to show you how to work with character strings.

```
CP/M  68000  Assembler          Revision 04.03        Page   1
Source File: B:STEP3.S

 1
 2
 3                              ***********************************************
 4                              ** Output of an ASCII line        step 3 **
 5                              ***********************************************
 6
 7
 8 00000000 3E3C0030                     move.w  #$30,d7        * ASCII null
 9
10 00000004 3F07            out:         move.w  d7,-(sp)       * character output
11 00000006 3F3C0002                     move.w  #2,-(sp)       * Code: CONOUT
12 0000000A 4E41                         trap    #1             * call GEMDOS
13 0000000C 588F                         addq.l  #4,sp          * stack correction
14
15 0000000E 5207                         addq.b  #1,d7          * new ASCII character
16
17 00000010 0C070039                     cmpi.b  #$39,d7        * = "9" (ASCII)
18 00000014 63EE                         bls     out            * Yes: next character
19
20 00000016 3F3C000D                     move.w  #13,-(sp)      * output CR
21 0000001A 3F3C0002                     move.w  #2,-(sp)       * Code: CONOUT
22 0000001E 4E41                         trap    #1             * call GEMDOS
23 00000020 588F                         addq.l  #4,sp          * stack correction
24
25 00000022 3F3C000A                     move.w  #10,-(sp)      * output LF
26 00000026 3F3C0002                     move.w  #2,-(sp)       * Code: CONOUT
27 0000002A 4E41                         trap    #1             * call GEMDOS
28 0000002C 588F                         addq.l  #4,sp          * stack correction
29
30 0000002E 3F3C0000                     move.w  #0,-(sp)       * Code: WARMSTART
31 00000032 4E41                         trap    #1             * call GEMDOS
32
33 00000034                              .end
```

185

The third step: loop processing

In our third example, we'll output several ASCII characters in a loop, and thereby become acquainted with loop structures within a machine language program.

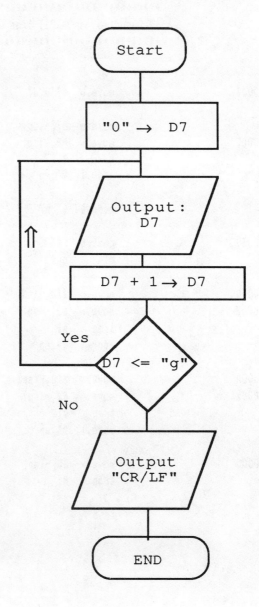

Let's output the digits 0 through 9 as a character string. To do this, in line 8 we first form the constant $30 (ASCII character zero) in data register D7. In lines 10-13 the character in D7 (still zero) is printed.

Next we form the next character (ASCII 1...9). Here we use the ADDQ (Add Quick) instruction of the 68000. This instruction allows the addition of a constant in the range 0-7 to the given destination. This instruction is comparable to the increment instruction of other processors. After execution of line 15, D7 contains the next ASCII value. Before we output this digit, we check to see if we have printed them all already. In the simplest form, we formulate a loop condition of "Repeat output as long as the digit is less than or equal to nine." We can see this logic in the flowchart.

In the machine language program, the loop condition is provided by lines 17 and 18. The comparison is made in line 17, wherein $39 corresponds to ASCII character 9 and the new ASCII value is in D7. The result of the comparison operation is tested in line 18 (for less than or equal to) and a branch is made to the label OUT if true, where a character is again printed. As you know, the BLS instruction is a relative branch instruction. you need not be concerned with the distance calculation, however. The assembler calculates the relative jump from the BLS instruction to the jump destination OUT itself.

The additional lines output a CR/LF and end the program.

The fourth step: line input and output

Our fourth example is an extension of the previous one, and a summary of everything we have learned so far. Here we want to read a line from the keyboard and output it again to the screen. New to this example is the temporary storage area to contain the string. This demonstrates the layout and management of variables. Take a look at the following flowchart and the machine language program pertaining to it.

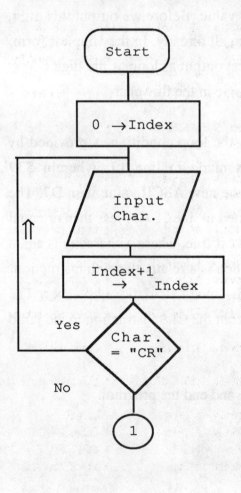

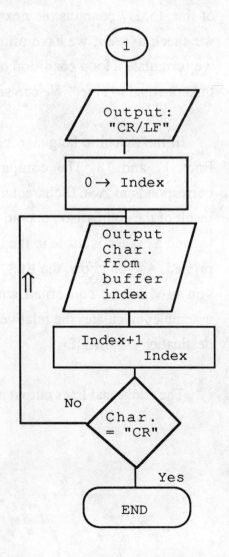

```
 1
 2
 3                              **********************************************
 4                              ** Input & Output of an ASCII char.   step 4 **
 5                              **********************************************
 6
 7
 8 00000000 2A7C0000004C                movea.l #line,a5        * set pointer
 9
10 00000006 3F3C0001          in:    move.w  #1,-(sp)        * Code: CONIN
11 0000000A 4E41                     trap    #1              * call GEMDOS
12 0000000C 548F                     addq.l  #2,sp           * stack correction
13
14 0000000E 1AC0                     move.b  d0,(a5)+        * save character
15
16 00000010 0C00000D                 cmpi.b  #13,d0          * was character a CR
17 00000014 66F0                     bne     in              * No: next character
18
19 00000016 3F3C000D                 move.w  #13,-(sp)       * output CR
20 0000001A 3F3C0002                 move.w  #2,-(sp)        * Code: CONOUT
21 0000001E 4E41                     trap    #1              * call GEMDOS
22 00000020 588F                     addq.l  #4,sp           * stack correction
23
24 00000022 3F3C000A                 move.w  #10,-(sp)       * output LF
25 00000026 3F3C0002                 move.w  #2,-(sp)        * Code: CONOUT
26 0000002A 4E41                     trap    #1              * call GEMDOS
27 0000002C 588F                     addq.l  #4,sp           * stack correction
28
29 0000002E 2A7C0000004C             movea.l #line,a5        * reset pointer
30
31 00000034 1E1D              out:   move.b  (a5)+,d7        * character from buffer
32
33 00000036 3F07                     move.w  d7,-(sp)        * output
34 00000038 3F3C0002                 move.w  #2,-(sp)        * Code: CONOUT
35 0000003C 4E41                     trap    #1              * call GEMDOS
36 0000003E 588F                     addq.l  #4,sp           * stack correction
37
38 00000040 0C07000D                 cmpi.b  #13,d7          * was character a CR
39 00000044 66EE                     bne     out             * No: more output
40 00000046                   .page
```

189

```
CP/M 68000 Assembler          Revision 04.03        Page  2
Source File: B:STEP4.S

41 00000046 3F3C0000                move.w  #0,-(sp)      * Code: WARMSTART
42 0000004A 4E41                     trap    #1            * call GEMDOS
43
44 0000004C                   line:  .ds.b 80              * 80 character buffer
45
46 0000009C                          .end
```

Let's start with line 44 of this example. Here an 80-byte memory area is reserved by the DS.B directive. We'll store the characters entered from the keyboard in this area, before we output them again. At the same time, in line 44 the symbol LINE is assigned the starting address of the storage area. Remember, this storage area is also called a buffer.

In line 8, a pointer is assigned to the start of this buffer. Address register A5 is loaded with the address of the buffer. We ll access the individual elements in the buffer by means of some instructions explained in the rest of this section.

First we'll concern ourselves with the input from the keyboard. A single character is read using the operating system function CONIN (console input, lines 10-12). The character is transferred to the buffer by the MOVE instruction in line 14. The addressing mode "address register indirect with postincrement" is used. The first character is placed at the address to which address register A5 indirectly points. After this transfer, A5 is incremented by 1 because we have selected "byte" as the operand format. The contents of the address register then point to the first free position within the line buffer after the first character is moved.

Since we want to input several characters, we must again make a loop for the console input. Please note that no output of the keyboard input is necessary within this loop in order to make the input immediately visible. The operating system function used automatically outputs the corresponding character on the screen. But still we must define suitable ending criteria for our loop.

As a general rule, input is always concluded with the <RETURN> key. When this key is pressed it returns the non-printable ASCII code CR, which we know from the previous examples. This also corresponds to the actual function of the key. In our example, this key should be interpreted as ending the input line. Correspondingly, we programmed the loop termination condition in lines 16 and 17 with this key. As long as the key pressed is not the <RETURN> key (ASCII code 13), the character is placed in the buffer and another character is read.

You might have noticed that we haven't expressly checked to see if the buffer is full. We have purposely avoided this question in order to keep the program simple. To avoid the problem of buffer overflow, we simply made the buffer somewhat larger than we expect we'll need. You may want to check this condition yourself.

Lines 19 to 27 output a CR/LF so that the cursor is set to the start of the next line before the buffer contents are printed.

Before we can output the buffer character by character, we must reset the buffer pointer to its first position (with line 29). This is again done with a MOVE instruction, in which address register A5 is loaded with the address of the buffer.

The instructions in lines 31 to 36 get a character from the buffer and print it on the screen using the operation system function CONOUT (console output).

Lines 31 through 36 deserve special consideration. A character, indirectly indicated by the address in address register A5, is moved from the buffer into data register D7 by the MOVE instruction in line 31. The address in address register A5 is incremented by 1 at the same time, in order to point to the next character in the buffer. The character is pushed onto the stack by the MOVE instruction in line 33 so that it can be printed by an operating system call in lines 34 and 36. It is not possible to move the character directly from the buffer to the stack with one instruction. As you know, only words or long words can be placed on the stack. But the characters are read byte by byte from our buffer. Since the 68000 requires that the operand width be the same for both the source and destination, you must process different data widths separately.

The output of the buffer area is again programmed in a loop. The CR character is again used as the end criterium, since it was also stored in the buffer during the input (lines 38 and 39). The instructions following end the program as usual.

The fifth step: binary output

Our next example represents another partial solution to our problem. We want to convert a binary number into an ASCII string. We assume that the number to be printed is found in data register D7. This number should be printed bit-by-bit as ASCII zeros and ones. Let's take a look at the flowchart for this problem and the machine language program below.

```
C P / M   6 8 0 0 0   A s s e m b l e r          Revision 04.03        Page   1
Source File: B:STEP5.S

  1
  2
  3                              ************************************************
  4                              ** Output of an Binary Number       step 5 **
  5                              ************************************************
  6
  7
  8 00000000 2E3C0000F0F0            move.l  #$f0f0,d7      * number to output
  9
 10 00000006 7C1F         binout: move.l  #31,d6         * place counter
 11
 12 00000008 3A3C0018     out:    move.w  #$18,d5        * ASCII zero/2
 13 0000000C E38F                 lsl.l   #1,d7          * isolate bit
 14 0000000E DB05                 addx.b  d5,d5          * form 0/1 ASCII
 15
 16 00000010 3F05                 move.w  d5,-(sp)       * output
 17 00000012 3F3C0002             move.w  #2,-(sp)       * Code: CONOUT
 18 00000016 4E41                 trap    #1             * call GEMDOS
 19 00000018 588F                 addq.l  #4,sp          * stack correction
 20
 21 0000001A 51CEFFEC             dbf     d6,out         * counter-1, test for
 22                                                                        =-1
 23 0000001E 3F3C0000             move.w  #0,-(sp)       * Code: WARMSTART
 24 00000022 4E41                 trap    #1             * call GEMDOS
 25
 26 00000024                      .end
```

193

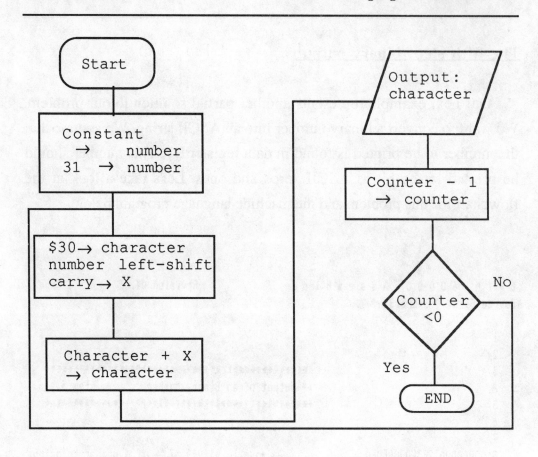

In line 8 we load a binary value into data register D7. Next we define a counter so that we can process the number bit by bit within the loop. This is necessary to determine when a binary number is completely printed. In binary representation it is normal to include leading zeros. Therefore we use D6 for the counter and set it to the constant 31 in line 10 of the program.

The constant 31 was chosen to enable us to use a special kind of loop. We actually want to process 32 bits. You might be tempted to use a counter from 0 to 32. But there is a special machine language instruction to decrement a data register (dx=dx-1) and compare the result. As long as the result is not -1, a branch is made to the top of the loop (line 12 and line 21). Another characteristic of the DBcc instruction is the conditional execution of the instruction. A condition code is first checked before the instruction is executed (similar to the DBcc instruction). The DBcc instruction is executed only as long as the cc-defined condition is *not* true. Since we won't be using this possibility in our example, we use F (false=never) as the condition code.

To output to the screen (which will be executed 32 times), we want to output one bit at a time within the loop. We'll output the most-significant bit first, and the least-significant bit last (let to right). The ASCII character is printed by lines 16 to 19 in the usual manner via an operating system call. The ASCII character printed (0 or 1) is dependent on the individual bits in data register D7. The generation the ASCII character is performed in lines 12-14, whereby the following computation rule is used.

The constant $18 is loaded into data register D5. This corresponds to one-half of ASCII zero ($30/2=$18). The reason we chose this constant will be made clear by the next instructions. We use the LSL instruction to prepare the next bit for output. This instruction shifts the bits within the register a given number of places. Zero bits are placed in the low order end of the register, and the left-most bits are shifted out the other end.

The last bit shifted is always copied to the X and C flags. Since we always want to output the next highest bit in the loop, we have chosen a shift left. We specify that we want to shift the register one place to the left.

After execution of the instruction, our bit (0 or 1) is found in the processor X flag. We use this to form our ASCII character. The ASCII code for zero is $30, and for one is $31. We can therefore form the ASCII code by adding the X flag to the constant $30. Unfortunately, there is no instruction that explicitly executes this operation. But there is an instruction that adds a source, a destination, and the X flag together. In this case the X flag is used as the carry bit in addition.

We form the constant $30 in line 12 and add $30 (in register D5), the constant $00, and the contents of the X-flag in line 14, by means of the ADDX instruction. To do this we must still form the constant $00 in the addition instruction. However, it would be much more practical to use the same register as both the source and destination. So we add $18, $18 again (=$30), and the X flag. The advantage is that the program is shorter and the instruction executes somewhat faster. The problem can be solved differently at program portions not requiring fast execution time, of course.

The sixth step: decimal to binary conversion

Except for inputting a decimal number, we have solved all problems of decimal to binary conversion. Before we tie all of the steps together into a complete program, we want to develop a method that processes decimal digits . As you have already noticed, we can enter a decimal number as strings of characters consisting of ASCII digits. For further processing, including the binary output, we must convert the input buffer to binary format. Here we use a simple rule of computation that we'll first present as a flowchart.

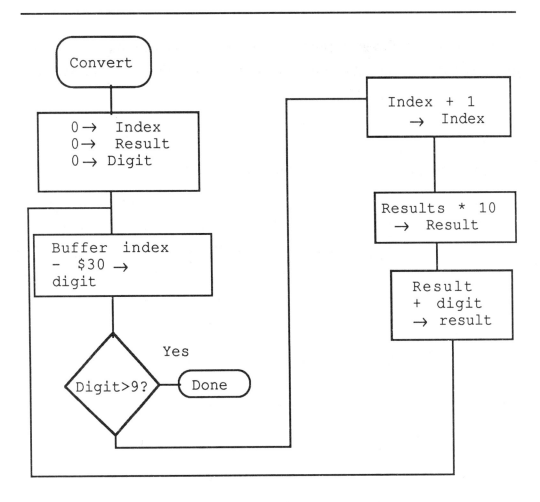

Before we take a look at the corresponding program, we want to clarify decimal to binary conversion. Let's take a look at a single decimal digit. It can be assigned the value 0 to 9. This corresponds to its binary coded decimal (BCD) value. An ASCII digit can be converted to BCD simply by subtracting the constant $30.

digit 0-9 = ASCII character $30-$39 = BCD value $00-$09

After converting the first digit we can view this as a temporary result. If a "non-digit character" follows the digit, we view the decimal number as

197

ended. To understand the conversion routine, let's take another look at the construction of a decimal number.

```
123 = 1 * 1000 +    result     0 * 10 + 1 = 1
      2 * 100 +     result     1 * 10 + 2 = 12
      3 * 10 +      result     12 * 10 + 3 = 123
      4 * 1 +       result     123 * 10 + 4 = 1234
```

We recognize that we need only multiply the previous conversion result (start=0) by 10, and then add the new digit, in order to get the converted number so far.

```
No.#    1234 digit 1    ASCII $31    BCD $01    result $0001
         234 digit 2    ASCII $32    BCD $02    result $000C
          34 digit 3    ASCII $33    BCD $03    result $007B
           4 digit 4    ASCII $34    BCD $04    result $04D2
```

This procedure is used in our example in lines 28 to 42. We'll describe the machine language procedure at the conclusion of the next listing.

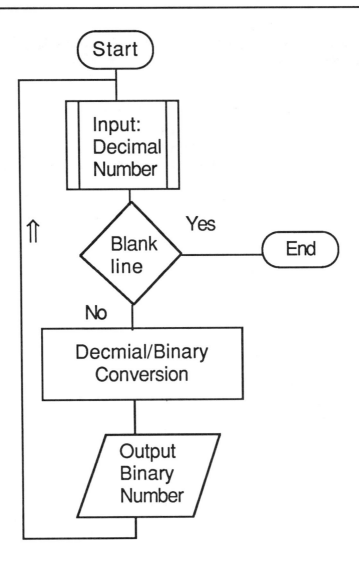

```
 1
 2
 3                        *************************************************
 4                        ** decinal/binary conversion        step 6 **
 5                        *************************************************
 6
 7
 8 00000000 2A7C0000006A            movea.l  #line,a5       * set up pointer
 9
10 00000006 3F3C0001    in:        move.w   #1,-(sp)       * Code: CONIN
11 0000000A 4E41                   trap     #1             * call GEMDOS
12 0000000C 548F                   addq.l   #2,sp          * stack correction
13 0000000E 1AC0                   move.b   d0,(a5)+       * save character
14
15 00000010 0C00000D               cmpi.b   #13,d0         * was character a CR
16 00000014 66F0                   bne      in             * No: next character
17
18 00000016 3F3C000D               move.w   #13,-(sp)      * output CR
19 0000001A 3F3C0002               move.w   #2,-(sp)       * Code: CONOUT
20 0000001E 4E41                   trap     #1             * call GEMDOS
21 00000020 588F                   addq.l   #4,sp          * stack correction
22
23 00000022 3F3C000A               move.w   #10,-(sp)      * output LF
24 00000026 3F3C0002               move.w   #2,-(sp)       * Code: CONOUT
25 0000002A 4E41                   trap     #1             * call GEMDOS
26 0000002C 588F                   addq.l   #4,sp          * stack correction
27
28 0000002E 2A7C0000006A           movea.l  #line,a5       * reset pointer
29
30 00000034 4287                   clr.l    d7             * clear result field
31 00000036 4286                   clr.l    d6             * clear digit
32
33 00000038 1C1D        convet:    move.b   (a5)+,d6       * process digit
34 0000003A 04060030               subi.b   #$30,d6        * ACII to BCD
35
36 0000003E 0C060009               cmpi.b   #9,d6          * BCD digit too large
37 00000042 6208                   bhi      binout         * Yes: no more digits
38
39 00000044 CEFC000A               mulu.w   #10,d7         * shift places
40 00000048 DE86                   add.l    d6,d7          * add digit
41 0000004A                .page
```

200

The above listing is the complete solution to our problem of decimal/binary conversion. We have three coherent function groups in our program:

- input of a line   (lines 8 to 26)
- conversion ASCII-binary   (lines 28 to 42)
- output a binary number   (lines 44 to 55)

Let's look at all the instructions in context. In line 8 a pointer (A5) is set to the input buffer. Lines 10-16 comprise the input loop. A character is read from the keyboard in lines 10 to 12. The function code (1) for the operating system function CONIN (console input) is placed on the stack by means of the MOVE instruction. The operating system is called by the TRAP instruction in the next line. The character is placed in the D0 register and moved to the buffer area by the next MOVE instruction, as long as a CR was not entered. Note that the buffer pointer is incremented to the next position in the buffer by the MOVE instruction.

Lines 18 to 26 set the cursor to the next line of the screen. A CR/LF control character is outputted in the usual way by means of the CONOUT (console output) function. First the control character is placed on the stack, followed by the function code for CONOUT (2). The operating system is called by the TRAP instruction. The parameters are subsequently removed from the stack by the manipulation of the stack pointer.

The number represented as an ASCII string and contained in the buffer is converted to a binary number (result in D7) in lines 28 to 42. The conversion rule is used to do this. First the pointer is set back to the first element in the buffer in line 28. Registers D7 and D6 are cleared (set to zero) in lines 30 and 31. The actual conversion loop begins at line 33.

A character is transferred from the input buffer to register D6, whereby the buffer pointer (A5) is simultaneously incremented by one byte. The ASCII digit is converted to a BCD number by subtracting the constant $30 in line 34. The result is checked for validity (line 36). If the result is greater than 9, the character is not a digit and the conversion is terminated (line 37). The previous result is increased by a power 10 as a result of a multiplication by 10 in line 39. The just-calculated position is added to the previous result in D7 (line 40). An absolute branch is made to the top of the loop with the BRA instruction in line 42.

The decimal/binary conversion is ended by the branch instruction in line 37. The program is continued in line 44. The decimal number entered is in register D7. This number is outputted as a binary number in the program segment from lines 44 to 55. Because our decimal conversion routine only works in the range 0..65535 ($0-$FFFF, determined by the multiplication instruction, which processes only words), we'll output only 16 places of the result. We have already explained how the output of a binary number works. We'll explain the function again after the last assembler listing.

In line 44 the counter in data register D6 is set to 15. The counter is then decremented by one until it becomes less then zero (DBF instruction in line 55). This corresponds to exactly 16 passes through the loop. Within this loop, the highest-order bit from the lower-order word in D7 is shifted into the X flag by means of the LSL instruction in line 47. In line 46 the constant $18, which corresponds to half of ASCII zero ($30/2=$18), is formed. This constant is added to itself by the addition in line 48, which corresponds to a multiplication by two. The contents of the X flag are also added in. Since the bit to be printed is contained in the X flag, the addition results in either a $30 or $31 in the D5 register. These values correspond to the ASCII characters for zero and one.

The result of this conversion in the D5 register is output to the screen in lines 50 to 53. With the instruction in line 50, the contents of the D5 register are pushed onto the stack. The function code 2 for the operating system function CONOUT is then formed. The operating system is called by means of the TRAP instruction and the character is printed. Finally, the stack pointer is corrected.

Once the loop is ended, the program continues with line 57. Here the function code for a warm start is generated and the operating system is called (line 58). This then ends the execution of the program.

Line 60 of the assembler listing contains the definition of the buffer area for the input loop.

The seventh step: the input loop

At the conclusion of this chapter, we want to refine our program . First we want to output a start message (prompt character) for input of the decimal number, and second, the whole routine should run in an input loop. This means that after one decimal/binary conversion is performed, another number is requested. Only when no number is entered will the program end.

On the following pages you find an extended flowchart and the assembler listing of the extended example program. We then will describe the assembler listing again.

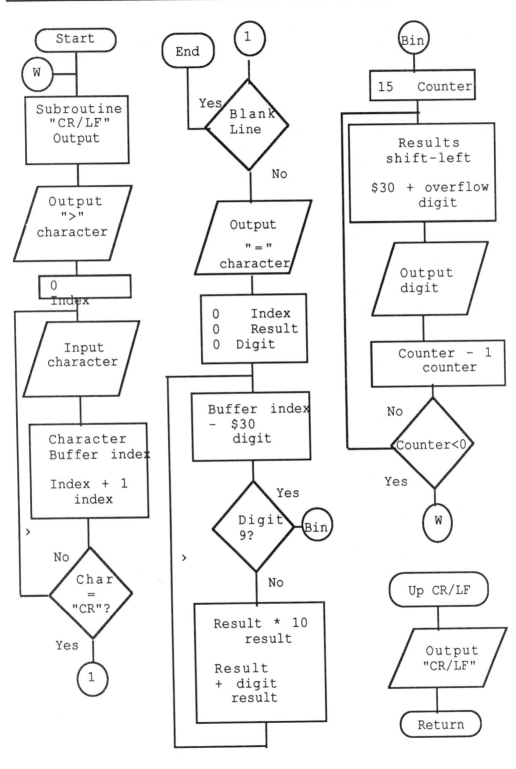

```
     1
     2
     3                            ************************************************
     4                            ** decimal/binary conversion & loop   step 7 **
     5                            ************************************************
     6
     7
     8 00000000 6174              loop:   bsr    crlf               * new line
     9
    10 00000002 3F3C203F                  move.w  #" ?",-(sp)        * prompt character
    11 00000006 3F3C0002                  move.w  #2,-(sp)           * Code: CONOUT
    12 0000000A 4E41                      trap    #1                 * call GEMDOS
    13 0000000C 588F                      addq.l  #4,sp              * stack correction
    14
    15 0000000E 2A7C00000090              movea.l #line,a5          * set up pointer
    16
    17 00000014 3F3C0001          in:     move.w  #1,-(sp)           * Code: CONIN
    18 00000018 4E41                      trap    #1                 * call GEMDOS
    19 0000001A 548F                      addq.l  #2,sp              * stack correction
    20
    21 0000001C 1AC0                      move.b  d0,(a5)+           * save character
    22
    23 0000001E 0C00000D                  cmpi.b  #13,d0             * is character a CR
    24 00000022 66F0                      bne     in                 * No: next character
    25
    26 00000024 BBFC00000091              cmpa.l  #line+1,a5         * test for blank
    27 0000002A 6744                      beq     end                * Yes: end program
    28
    29 0000002C 3F3C203D                  move.w  #" =",-(sp)        * delimeter
    30 00000030 3F3C0002                  move.w  #2,-(sp)           * Code: CONOUT
    31 00000034 4E41                      trap    #1                 * call GEMDOS
    32 00000036 588F                      addq.l  #4,sp              * stack correction
    33
    34 00000038 2A7C00000090              movea.l #line,a5          * reset pointer
    35
    36 0000003E 4287                      clr.l   d7                 * result field
    37 00000040 4286                      clr.l   d6                 * calc. field (remain
    38
    39 00000042 1C1D              convet: move.b  (a5)+,d6           * process digit
    40 00000044 04060030                  subi.b  #$30,d6            * ASCII to BCD
    41 00000048                   .page
```

```
42 00000048 0C060009              cmpi.b  #9,d6           * BCD digit too large
43 0000004C 6208                  bhi     binout          * Yes: no more digits
44
45 0000004E CEFC000A              mulu.w  #10,d7          * shift places
46 00000052 DE86                  add.l   d6,d7           * add digits
47
48 00000054 60EC                  bra     convet          * new digit
49
50 00000056 7C0F        binout:   move.l  #15,d6          * place counter
51
52 00000058 3A3C0018    out:      move.w  #$18,d5         * ASCII zero/2
53 0000005C E34F                  lsl.w   #1,d7           * isolate bit
54 0000005E DB05                  addx.b  d5,d5           * form ASCII 0/1
55
56 00000060 3F05                  move.w  d5,-(sp)        * output
57 00000062 3F3C0002              move.w  #2,-(sp)        * Code: CONOUT
58 00000066 4E41                  trap    #1              * call GEMDOS
59 00000068 588F                  addq.l  #4,sp           * stack correction
60
61 0000006A 51CEFFEC              dbf     d6,out          * counter-1, test for
62
63 0000006E 6090                  bra loop                * new input
64
65 00000070 3F3C0000    end:      move.w  #0,-(sp)        * Code: WARMSTART
66 00000074 4E41                  trap    #1              * call GEMDOS
67
68 00000076 3F3C000D    crlf:     move.w  #13,-(sp)       * output CR
69 0000007A 3F3C0002              move.w  #2,-(sp)        * Code: CONOUT
70 0000007E 4E41                  trap    #1              * call GEMDOS
71 00000080 588F                  addq.l  #4,sp           * stack correction
72
73 00000082 3F3C000A              move.w  #10,-(sp)       * output LF
74 00000086 3F3C0002              Move.w  #2,-(sp)        * Code: CONOUT
75 0000008A 4E41                  trap    #1              * call GEMDOS
76 0000008C 588F                  addq.l  #4,sp           * stack correction
77
78 0000008E 4E75                  rts                     * return
79
80 00000090              line:    .ds.b 80                * 80 character buffer
81
82 000000E0                       .end
```

The first visible change in our program concerns the output of CR/LF. We have used this function as a subroutine. The subroutine is defined in lines 68 to 78; its function is identical to that in our previous examples.

This subroutine is called in line 8. It is not used at any other place in the program; it serves only to demonstrate the BSR and RTS instructions. The prompt character (?) is printed with lines 10 to 13. The CONOUT function of the operating system again is used to do this. A special feature is found in line 10, where we define the character to be printed by means of a text constant. Here we have to get around an inadequacy of the assembler. The operand width of the MOVE instruction is defined as "word." If you specify only an ASCII character, it is expanded to word width by the assembler. It does this by appending a $00 on the right. But this means that character is no longer in the lower-order portion of the word, meaning that no visible character is printed. The output functions correctly, but $00 is not a printable character.

We can get around this inadequacy of the assembler by defining the text constant as two characters, namely a space and an ASCII character. The assembler then generates a word, with its lower byte containing the ASCII character. This trick is not very "clean," since the higher-order portion is always supposed to contain binary zero in order to maintain compatibility with future operating systems. But since we have formulated our example specifically for the ST, we'll overlook this minor defect.

Lines 15 through 24 process the input of a line. The use of this function does not differ from out previous example.

Lines 26 and 27 are added at this point. Here we check if a decimal number was actually entered. This is done by simply testing the buffer pointer (A5) to see if it points to the second element in the buffer. If this is the case, only a single character is in the buffer. Since the last character in the buffer is always a CR, we can assume that if the buffer contains only one character, no digits have been entered. If a blank line is recognized, a branch is made directly to the end processing (lines 65 and 66). There the program is exited to the operating system in the usual manner.

If the line entered is not blank, a delimiter is created in lines 29 to 32 that separates the input number from the output. We again use the operating system function CONOUT.

The decimal/binary conversion is executed in lines 34 to 48. Because we have described this function in the previous examples, we'll not repeat ourselves here. The same applies to the binary output in lines 50 to 61.

In line 63 we have an unconventional branch instruction, "back to input." This concluded our input loop. A prompt character is printed on the next line and the program waits for input. The program can be ended only by a processor reset or by pressing <RETURN>.

Here we'll end our "step-by-step" introduction of assembly programming. In the next chapter we'll present somewhat larger assembly language programs, but won't go into such detail of their development.

Chapter Eight

Solutions to Typical Problems

- •Introduction
- •Hexadecimal/decimal conversion
- •Decimal/hexadecimal conversion
- •Calculating an average
- •Simple sorting
- •Output: Strings
- •Input: Strings with check
- •Output: Date
- •Factorial calculation

```
┌─────────────────────────┐
│     Introduction        │
└─────────────────────────┘
```

In this chapter we'll present some more example programs and use them to illustrate some programming techniques and operating system functions. We will also present some typical algorithms.

We could use more "powerful" operating system functions at certain places and thereby make our example programs shorter. The goal of this book, however, is to explain the methodology of assembly language programming and to practice it using examples. For a more complete discussion of the GEM-DOS operating system routines you might want to refer to the Atari ST Gem Programmer's Reference from Abacus.

Each example is divided into several parts. As an introduction we will familiarize you with the statement of the problem and suggest ways of solving it. Following this will be a flowchart and a complete assembly language listing. This and the algorithms used will then be explained.

We recommend that you try to understand the examples. If you own an assembler, you can try out all of them with the ST.

Hexadecimal/decimal conversion

The problem of hex/decimal conversion is quite similar to the decimal/binary conversion which we presented in the previous chapter. Hexadecimal numbers are also just a representation form for values, using "16" as the number base. Corresponding to this there are also 16 digits in the hexadecimal system. These digits are represented by the normal digits 0-9 and the letters A-F.

In the next program example we'll show you how to convert hexadecimal numbers to decimal. Here we'll use two basic algorithms. These concern the conversion of a hexadecimal string to binary register contents and outputting the register contents as a decimal string (decimal number).

The conversion of a hexadecimal number to register format is relatively easy to understand. Each digit corresponds exactly to the possible bit combinations of four bits within a binary number.

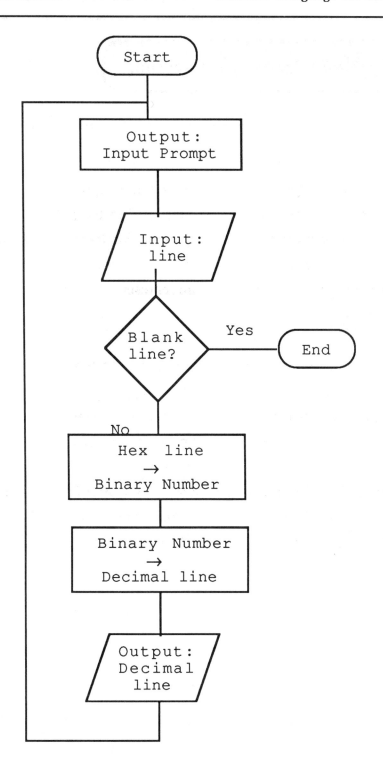

CP/M 68000 Assembler   Revision 04.03   Page 1
Source File: B:EXP1.S

```
 1
 2
 3                          *********************************************
 4                          * Hexadecimal/Decimal conversion  Example 1*
 5                          *********************************************
 6
 7
 8 00000000 610000C8        loop:   bsr     crlf            * Cursor new line
 9
10 00000004 3F3C203F                move.w  #" ?",-(sp)     * Prompt char
11 00000008 3F3C0002                move.w  #2,-(sp)        * Code: CONOUT
12 0000000C 4E41                    trap    #1              * Call GEMDOS
13 0000000E 588F                    addq.l  #4,sp           * Stack correction
14
15 00000010 2A7C000000E4            movea.l #line,a5        * Set pointer
16
17 00000016 3F3C0001        in:     move.w  #1,-(sp)        * Cod: CONIN
18 0000001A 4E41                    trap    #1              * Call GEMDOS
19 0000001C 548F                    addq.l  #2,sp           * Stack correction
20
21 0000001E 1AC0                    move.b  d0,(a5)+        *save character
22
23 00000020 0C00000D                cmpi.b  #13,d0          * char a "CR"?
24 00000024 66F0                    bne     in              *N: next character
25
26 00000026 BBFC000000E5            cmpa.l  #line+1,a5      * Test for blank
27 0000002C 67000096                beq     end             * Y: program end
28
29 00000030 2A7C000000E4            movea.l #line,a5        * Reset pointer
30
31 00000036 42B7                    clr.l   d7              *clr. result field
32 00000038 42B6                    clr.l   d6              * calc. field(rem)
33
34 0000003A 1C1D            convet: move.b  (a5)+,d6        * process digit
35 0000003C 0C060030                cmpi.b  #$30,d6         * Ctrl. char.
36 00000040 6536                    blo     decout          * Y: end conv.
37
38 00000042 04060030                subi.b  #$30,d6         * ACCII to BCD
39 00000046 0C060009                cmpi.b  #9,d6           * BCD digit OK
40 0000004A 6310                    bls     ok              * Y: was digit
41 0000004C                 .page
```

```
42 0000004C 04060027              subi.b  ##$27,d6       #BCD digit correct
43
44 00000050 0C06000A              cmpi.b  ##$a,d6        * Letter OK
45 00000054 6522                  blo     decout         * N:  convert
46
47 00000056 0C06000F              cmpi.b  ##$f,d6        * Letter OK
48 0000005A 621C                  bhi     decout         * N: end convert
49
50 0000005C E98F          ok:     lsl.l   #4,d7          * place shift
51 0000005E DE86                  add.l   d6,d7          * add digit
52
53 00000060 0C870000FFFF          cmpi.l  ##$ffff,d7     * test overflow
54 00000066 63D2                  bls     convet         * N: new digit
55
56 00000068 6160                  bsr     crlf           * cursor new
57 0000006A 3F3C2021              move.w  #" !",-(sp)    * error message
58 0000006E 3F3C0002              move.w  #2,-(sp)       * Code CONOUT
59 00000072 4E41                  trap    #1             * Call GEMDOS
60 00000074 588F                  addq.l  #4,sp          * Stack correction
61
62 00000076 6088                  bra     loop           * input new number
63
64
65 00000078 6150          decout: bsr     crlf           #cursor new line
66
67 0000007A 3F3C203D              move.w  #" =",-(sp)    * result message
68 0000007E 3F3C0002              move.w  #2,-(sp)       * Code: CONOUT
69 00000082 4E41                  trap    #1             * Call GEMDOS
70 00000084 588F                  addq.l  #4,sp          * Stack correction
71
72 00000086 02870000FFFF          andi.l  ##$ffff,d7     * limit places
73
74 0000008C 2A7C000000E4          movea.l #line,a5       * Set pointer
75
76 00000092 2C07          dodec:  move.l  d7,d6          * process digit
77
78 00000094 8CFC000A              divu.w  #10,d6         * form value/10
79 00000098 3E06                  move.w  d6,d7          * save results
80 0000009A 4846                  swap    d6             * form remainder
81 0000009C 06460030              addi.w  ##$30,d6       * generate ASCII
82 000000A0              .page
```

217

```
 83 000000A0 1AC6                    move.b  d6,(a5)+       * digit in buffer
 84
 85 000000A2 0C470000                cmpi.w  #0,d7          * all digits?
 86 000000A6 66EA                    bne     dodec          * Y: done new *
 87
 88 000000A8 BBFC000000E4    out:    cmpa.l  #line,a5       * test buffer
 89 000000AE 6700FF50                beq     loop           * Y: done new *
 90
 91 000000B2 1E25                    move.b  -(a5),d7       * get character
 92 000000B4 024700FF                andi.w  #$ff,d7        * normal char.
 93
 94 000000B8 3F07                    move.w  d7,-(sp)       * output char
 95 000000BA 3F3C0002                move.w  #2,-(sp)       * Code: CONOUT
 96 000000BE 4E41                    trap    #1             * Call GEMDOS
 97 000000C0 588F                    addq.l  #4,sp          * Stack correction
 98
 99 000000C2 60E4                    bra     out            * test if done
100
101
102 000000C4 3F3C0000        end:    move.w  #0,-(sp)       * Code WARMSTART
103 000000C8 4E41                    trap    #1             * Call GEMDOS
104
105
106 000000CA 3F3C000D        crlf:   move.w  #13,-(sp)      * Output CR
107 000000CE 3F3C0002                move.w  #2,-(sp)       * Code: CONOUT
108 000000D2 4E41                    trap    #1             * Call GEMDOS
109 000000D4 588F                    addq.l  #4,sp          * Stack correction
110
111 000000D6 3F3C000A                move.w  #10,-(sp)      * Output LF
112 000000DA 3F3C0002                move.w  #2,-(sp)       * Code: CONOUT
113 000000DE 4E41                    trap    #1             * Call GEMDOS
114 000000E0 588F                    addq.l  #4,sp          * Stack correction
115
116 000000E2 4E75                    rts                    * Return
117
118
119 000000E4            line:    .ds.b 80                   * 80 char buffer
120
121 00000134                     .end
```

218

We need only convert the hex digit in ASCII form to the corresponding bit pattern. The orderliness of the ASCII code helps us here.

Binary 0000 to 1001 (0-9 hexadecimal) = ASCII $30-39

Binary 1010 to 1111 (A-F hexadecimal) = ASCII $41-$46

We can derive a computational rule from this ordered ASCII code:

If the hex digit is in the range from ASCII 0-9, we subtract $30 in order to get the binary value. If the hex digit is in the range from ASCII code A-F, we subtract $37 in order to get the binary value. If the digit is not within one of these two ranges, we assume that the hexadecimal number is ended. If a digit occurs, we multiply the previous result by 16 (shift it four bits to the left) and add the new digit to it.

The algorithm for binary/decimal conversion is somewhat more complicated in theory, but it is very easy to realize on the 68000. The computation rule used is based on the Horner method. Here a number to be converted is divided by the new base (here 10). The remainder of the division corresponds to a digit in the given system (0-9). This division is continued until the result becomes zero. An example will clarify this.

```
$04D2  (# 1234) / $A (# 10)  = $7B (#123)          rem 4
$007B  (#  123) / $A (# 10)  = $0C (# 12)          rem 3
$000C  (#   12) / $A (# 10)  = $01 (#  1)          rem 2
$0001  (#    1) / $A (# 10)  = $00 (#  0)          rem 1
```

We recognize that we get all of the places of the decimal number with this method, but in the reverse order. Therefore we must store all of the digits and then output then in the proper order after the conversion.

We now turn to a description of the machine language program:

In line 8, the subroutine for creating a CR/LF is called. This is programmed in lines 106 to 116. Its function is identical to the subroutine in the last example. The instructions in lines 106 to 109 output a CR on the screen. The GEM-DOS routine CONOUT is used for this. Lines 111 to 114 output an LF by the same procedure. The subroutine is ended by the RTS instruction in line 116.

Lines 10-13 output a "?" on the screen as the input prompt. The GEM-DOS console output function CONOUT is again used. In line 6, the input buffer pointer is initialized. It then points to the first byte in this area. The input area itself is defined in line 119. In our example it can hold up to 80 characters.

Lines 15 to 24 form the input loop. The operating system is called in lines 17 to 19. Here we use the GEM-DOS console input function CONIN, with which you are already acquainted. Line 21 places the character entered into the input buffer. The ASCII code of the key is then passed in the lower byte of the D0 register. The end condition for the input loop is tested in lines 23 and 24. As long as the D0 register does not contain a CR, the loop (input) is continued with the instruction in line 17. The next character is then read.

If the last character was a CR (<RETURN> key), the program continues execution with the instruction in line 26. Here the input buffer is tested to see if it contains only one character. If this is the case, the program branches to the instruction in line 102. There the program is ended with the usual operating system call.

If the line was not blank, execution continues with line 29. The conversion routine which converts the contents of the input buffer to a binary number starts here. First a pointer is set back to the first byte in the buffer in line 29. Two data registers are initialized (set to zero) in lines 31 and 32 according to our rule of computation for the hex/binary conversion and our flowchart. We will use D7 as the result field and D6 as the calculation field for a hex digit.

The processing of hex digits starts at line 34 (within the loop). The instruction in line 34 moves a hex digit from the buffer to the calculation field (D6) and sets the pointer (A5) to the next field. Some of the possible non-hex-digit characters are filtered out by the comparison instruction in line 35. If a character is smaller than $30, it can only be a control character or special character. In this case, a branch is made to the decimal output routine (at line 65) via the instruction in line 36. If the ASCII character is greater than $30, $30 is subtracted, regardless of the fact that the character still may not be a hex digit. The comparison instruction in line 79 determines whether or not the character is a digit from 0-9. If it is, a branch is made to the instruction in line 50 where this digit is processed. If the character is not in the group 0-9, the conversion in line 43 is made. Here the constant $27 is subtracted. Remember that we have already subtracted $30 from the original ASCII character. Now the result must be in the range from $A to $F, which corresponds to the second group of hex digits. This condition is checked in lines 44 through 48. If the character is not in this group either, the program continues with the decimal output. Otherwise, the correctly converted digit is processed at line 50.

The `LSL.L` instruction in line 50 shifts the previous result field four bits to the left. Then the new hex digit is added to the result field (line 51).

The result is checked at the end of the end of the conversion loop (line 53). If the result field is less than $FFFF, the conversion continues with the next digit. This is done by a branch back to the top of the loop (line 34). If an overflow occurs, the cursor is set to the to the start of the next line by a call to the CR/LF subroutine in line 56 and the instructions in lines 57 to 60 print an exclamation point (!) as an error message. The conversion is not continued any further. The program branches to the start of the program in the event of an error (line 62).

The decimal output routine starts at line 65. Here too we use the same algorithm which we described earlier and which we defined in the flowchart. First the cursor is moved down a line by a call to the CR/LF subroutine in line 65 and the equals sign (=) is printed in lines 67-70.

The instructions in lines 72 and 74 prepare the output corresponding to our algorithm. The output value is limited to binary numbers in range 0-65535 and the pointer (A5) is set to the start of the buffer area. This is now used not for entering a string, but as temporary storage for the result of the Horner method.

The decimal digits are calculated starting with the instruction in line 76. The initial value is divided by 10 in line 78. The integer result is stored as the new value in register D7, where it will remain for the next pass through the loop and be used as the initial value for the next digit. The upper and lower halves of the register are exchanged by the SWAP instruction in line 80. The remainder of the division is stored in the higher-order portion, which already corresponds to a "finished" digit. The ASCII code is generated by adding the constant $30 (line 81). The result is placed in the buffer (line 83), whereby the address counter is incremented by one byte.

A branch is made to the start of the conversion routine in line 86. The output of all decimal digits must be realized by the routine from lines 88 to 99. First a test is made to see if all the characters have been printed already. If the buffer is empty, a execution branches to the start of the program. Otherwise a character is fetched from the buffer, the pointer is incremented, the word is masked, and the character is printed (CONOUT). The loop is continued by a branch to its start (line 99). It can be exited only through the condition in line 89.

You will see parts of this program again and again in our examples. Naturally, we will not describe identical program parts each time they occur.

Decimal/hexadecimal conversion

The problem of decimal to hexadecimal conversion is the reverse of the hex/decimal conversion which we presented in the previous section. Here again we will use two basic algorithms. These are a conversion of a decimal string to a binary number and outputting this binary number as a hexadecimal string.

We have already explained the processing of decimal numbers entered via the keyboard in the previous chapter (decimal/binary conversion). The new part of this problem is the output of hexadecimal numbers. The algorithm we use is easy to understand if you recall the previous example (hex/decimal conversion). To output a hex number, the binary contents of a register are simply divided into groups of four bits. This division is accomplished through logical SHIFT operations. Each group of 4 bits corresponds to one hex digit. These hex digits must be converted to ASCII characters before they can be printed. This is done simply by adding constants. First $30 is added in order to generate the digits 0-9 (ASCII $30-$39). If the result is greater than $39, the previous result is extended to the hex digits A-F (ASCII $61-$66) by adding $27.

Let us take a look at the flowchart and the assembler listing for the decimal/hexadecimal conversion:

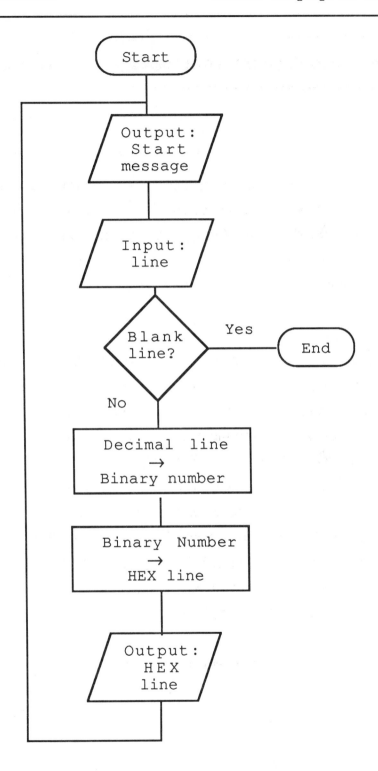

```
 1
 2
 3                              ********************************************
 4                              * Hexadecimal/Decimal conversion  Example 2*
 5                              ********************************************
 6
 7
 8 00000000 610000BC        loop:   bsr     crlf            * Cursor new line
 9
10 00000004 3F3C203F                move.w  #" ?",-(sp)      * Prompt char
11 00000008 3F3C0002                move.w  #2,-(sp)        * Code: CONOUT
12 0000000C 4E41                    trap    #1              * Call GEMDOS
13 0000000E 588F                    addq.l  #4,sp           * Stack correction
14
15 00000010 2A7C000000D8            movea.l #line,a5        * Set pointer
16
17 00000016 3F3C0001        in:     move.w  #1,-(sp)        * Cod: CONIN
18 0000001A 4E41                    trap    #1              * Call GEMDOS
19 0000001C 548F                    addq.l  #2,sp           * Stack correction
20
21 0000001E 1AC0                    move.b  d0,(a5)+        #save character
22
23 00000020 0C00000D                cmpi.b  #13,d0          * char a "CR"?
24 00000024 66F0                    bne     in              *N: next character
25
26 00000026 BBFC000000D9            cmpa.l  #line+1,a5      * Test for blank
27 0000002C 670000BA                beq     end             * Y: program end
28
29 00000030 2A7C000000D8            movea.l #line,a5        * Reset pointer
30
31 00000036 4287                    clr.l   d7              #clr. result field
32 00000038 4286                    clr.l   d6              * calc. field(rem)
33
34 0000003A 1C1D            convet: move.b  (a5)+,d6        * process digit
35 0000003C 04060030                subi.b  #$30,d6         * ACCII to BCD
36
37 00000040 0C060009                cmpi.b  #9,d6           * BCD digit OK
38 00000044 621E                    bhi     hexout          * Y: no more digit
39 00000046                 .page
```

```
C P / M   6 8 0 0 0   A s s e m b l e r        Revision 04.03        Page   2
Source File: B:EXP2.S

40 00000046 CEFC000A              mulu.w  #10,d7          * place shift
41 0000004A DE86                  add.l   d6,d7           * add digits
42
43 0000004C 0C870000FFFF          cmpi.l  #$ffff,d7       * test overflow
44 00000052 63E6                  bls     convet          * N: new digit
45
46 00000054 6168                  bsr     crlf            * cursor new line
47
48 00000056 3F3C2021              move.w  #" !",-(sp)      * error message
49 0000005A 3F3C0002              move.w  #2,-(sp)         * Code CONOUT
50 0000005E 4E41                  trap    #1              * Call GEMDOS
51 00000060 588F                  addq.l  #4,sp           * Stack correction
52
53 00000062 609C                  bra     loop            * input new number
54
55
56
57 00000064 6158         hexout:  bsr     crlf            * cursor new line
58
59 00000066 3F3C203D              move.w  #" =",-(sp)      * result message
60 0000006A 3F3C0002              move.w  #2,-(sp)         * Code: CONOUT
61 0000006E 4E41                  trap    #1              * Call GEMDOS
62 00000070 588F                  addq.l  #4,sp           * Stack correction
63
64 00000072 02870000FFFF          andi.l  #$ffff,d7       * limit places
65
66 00000078 2A7C000000D8          movea.l #line,a5        * Set pointer
67
68 0000007E 2C07         dohex:   move.l  d7,d6           * process digit
69 00000080 0246000F              andi.w  #$f,d6          * mask value
70 00000084 E84F                  lsr.w   #4,d7           * form remanider
71 00000086 06460030              addi.w  #$30,d6         * generate ASCII
72
73 0000008A 0C460039              cmpi.w  #$39,d6         * letter
74 0000008E 6304                  bls     ok              * N; digit ok
75
76 00000090 06460027              addi.w  #$27,d6         * correct digit
77 00000094                       .page
```

```
78 00000094 1AC6         ok:     move.b  d6,(a5)+      * digit in buffer
79
80 00000096 0C470000             cmpi.w  #0,d7         * all digits?
81 0000009A 66E2                 bne     dohex         * Y: new digit
82
83 0000009C BBFC000000D8 out:    cmpa.l  #line,a5      * test buffer
84 000000A2 6700FF5C             beq     loop          * Y: done new #
85
86 000000A6 1E25                 move.b  -(a5),d7      * get character
87 000000A8 024700FF             andi.w  #$ff,d7       * normal char.
88
89 000000AC 3F07                 move.w  d7,-(sp)      * output char
90 000000AE 3F3C0002             move.w  #2,-(sp)      * Code: CONOUT
91 000000B2 4E41                 trap    #1            * Call GEMDOS
92 000000B4 588F                 addq.l  #4,sp         * Stack correction
93
94 000000B6 60E4                 bra     out           * test if done
95
96
97 000000B8 3F3C0000     end:    move.w  #0,-(sp)      * Code WARMSTART
98 000000BC 4E41                 trap    #1            * Call GEMDOS
99
100
101 000000BE 3F3C000D    crlf:   move.w  #13,-(sp)     * Output CR
102 000000C2 3F3C0002            move.w  #2,-(sp)      * Code: CONOUT
103 000000C6 4E41                trap    #1            * Call GEMDOS
104 000000C8 588F                addq.l  #4,sp         * Stack correction
105
106 000000CA 3F3C000A            move.w  #10,-(sp)     * Output LF
107 000000CE 3F3C0002            move.w  #2,-(sp)      * Code: CONOUT
108 000000D2 4E41                trap    #1            * Call GEMDOS
109 000000D4 588F                addq.l  #4,sp         * Stack correction
110
111 000000D6 4E75                rts                   * Return
112
113
114 000000D8         line:   .ds.b 80                  * 80 char buffer
115
116
117 00000128                     .end
```

The decimal/hex conversion starts in lines 8 to 13 with the output of "CR/LF" and a question mark as the input prompt character. The CR/LF is outputted by a subroutine defined in lines 101 to 111. Lines 15 through 24 get an input line from the keyboard into the buffer. This is defined in line 114. The buffer is then checked (lines 26 and 27) to see if it contains a blank line and if so, the program is ended in lines 97 and 98.

If characters are present in the buffer, it is converted to a binary register value (D7) by the routine in lines 29 to 53.

The output of the hex number, now contained in D7, starts in line 57. First the cursor is set to the start of the next screen line by outputting a CR/LF. Our subroutine at line 101 is used for this purpose. An equals sign is printed to indicate that the hex number follows (lines 59 to 62) and the contents of higher-order portion of D7 are masked out (line 64).

A hex digit is processed in line 66. First a copy is of the number to be printed (D7) is placed in register D6. The all but the lower 4 bits are masked out of this register (line 69). The number being processed in the D7 register is shifted 4 bit positions to the right (line 70) because these bits are now in register D6. These bits are then converted to a hex digit according to our rule of computation.

The constant $30 is added in line 71 and a test is made to see if the character is a digits from 0-9 (line 73). If this is the case, the D6 register can be printed as a hex digit (at line 78). Otherwise the constant $27 is added (line 76).

The output at line 78 does not go directly to the screen, but first to the buffer, which must then be printed in reverse order after the conversion. But first the number in the D7 register is checked to see if all the necessary places have been processed (lines 80 to 81) and a branch is made to the top of the loop if necessary (line 68). If the number has been completely converted, it is printed in lines 83 to 94. A branch is made to the start of the program (input loop at line 8) when the output is done.

Calculating an average

With this example we want to explain the processing elements of a simple table, and so we leave the topic of simple input and output.

Decimal numbers are entered and stored as elements of a table. When the first blank line is entered, the program calculates the average (integer value) of the previous values and outputs the result in decimal.

First take a look at the flowchart and the assembler listing of the average calculation program:

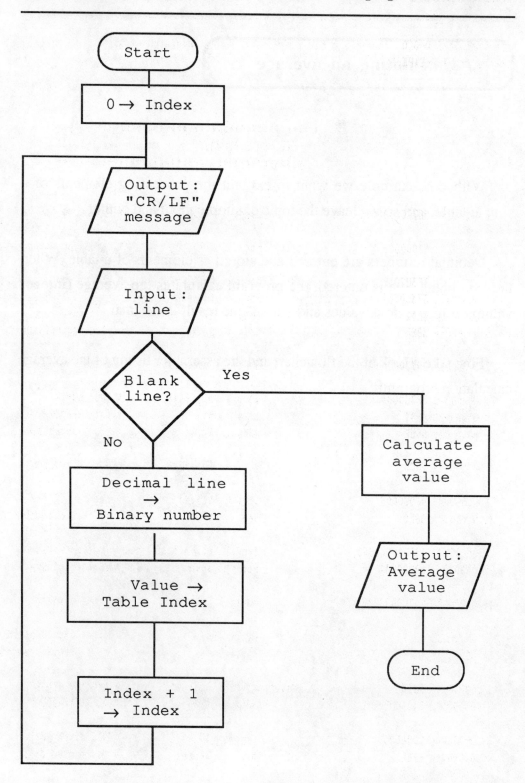

CP/M 68000 Assembler   Revision 04.03   Page 1
Source File: B:EXP3.S

```
 1
 2
 3                              ********************************************
 4                              * CALCULATE AVERAGE                Example 3*
 5                              ********************************************
 6
 7
 8 00000000 287C00000144                movea.l  #tab,a4        * Data area for #s
 9
10 00000006 610000B6          loop:     bsr      crlf           * Cursor new line
11
12 0000000A 3F3C203F                    move.w   #" ?",-(sp)    * Prompt char
13 0000000E 3F3C0002                    move.w   #2,-(sp)       * Code: CONOUT
14 00000012 4E41                        trap     #1             * Call GEMDOS
15 00000014 588F                        addq.l   #4,sp          * Stack correction
16
17 00000016 2A7C000000F4                movea.l  #line,a5       * Set pointer
18
19 0000001C 3F3C0001          in:       move.w   #1,-(sp)       * Cod: CONIN
20 00000020 4E41                        trap     #1             * Call GEMDOS
21 00000022 548F                        addq.l   #2,sp          * Stack correction
22
23 00000024 1AC0                        move.b   d0,(a5)+       * save character
24
25 00000026 0C00000D                    cmpi.b   #13,d0         * char a "CR"?
26 0000002A 66F0                        bne      in             * N: next character
27
28 0000002C BBFC000000F5                cmpa.l   #line+1,a5     * Test for blank
29 00000032 670000A4                    beq      summ           * Y:generate sum
30
31 00000036 2A7C000000F4                movea.l  #line,a5       * Reset pointer
32
33 0000003C 4287                        clr.l    d7             * clear result field
34 0000003E 4286                        clr.l    d6             * calc. field(remainde
35
36 00000040 1C1D              convet:   move.b   (a5)+,d6       * process digit
37 00000042 04060030                    subi.b   #$30,d6        * ACCII to BCD
38
39 00000046 0C060009                    cmpi.b   #9,d6          * BCD digit OK
40 0000004A 621E                        bhi      proces         * Y: no more digit
41 0000004C                   .page
```

```
42 0000004C CEFC000A              mulu.w  #10,d7           * place shift
43 00000050 DE86                  add.l   d6,d7            * add digit
44
45 00000052 0C870000FFFF          cmpi.l  #$ffff,d7        * test for carry
46 00000058 63E6                  bls     convet           * N: new digit
47
48 0000005A 6162                  bsr     crlf             * cursor new line
49
50 0000005C 3F3C2021              move.w  #" !",-(sp)      * error message
51 00000060 3F3C0002              move.w  #2,-(sp)         * Code CONOUT
52 00000064 4E41                  trap    #1               * Call GEMDOS
53 00000066 588F                  addq.l  #4,sp            * Stack correction
54
55 00000068 609C                  bra     loop             * enter new #
56
57
58 0000006A 38C7          proces: move.w  d7,(a4)+         * value in table
59
60 0000006C 6098                  bra     loop             * enter new line
61
62
63 0000006E 3F3C203D      decout: move.w  #" =",-(sp)      * result message
64 00000072 3F3C0002              move.w  #2,-(sp)         * Code: CONOUT
65 00000076 4E41                  trap    #1               * Call GEMDOS
66 00000078 588F                  addq.l  #4,sp            * Stack correction
67
68 0000007A 02870000FFFF          andi.l  #$ffff,d7        * limit places
69
70 00000080 2A7C000000F4          movea.l #line,a5         * Set pointer
71
72 00000086 2C07          dodec:  move.l  d7,d6            * process digit
73 00000088 8CFC000A              divu.w  #10,d6           * form value/10
74 0000008C 3E06                  move.w  d6,d7            * save results
75 0000008E 4846                  swap.w  d6               * form remainder
76 00000090 06460030              addi.w  #$30,d6          * generate ASCII
77 00000094 1AC6                  move.b  d6,(a5)+         * digit in buffer
78
79 00000096 0C470000              cmpi.w  #0,d7            * all digits?
80 0000009A 66EA                  bne     dodec            * N; next digit
81 0000009C              .page
```

234

```
82 0000009C BBFC000000F4    out:    cmpa.l  #line,a5        * test buffer
83 000000A2 6602            bne     nzlf            * N: all digits
84
85 000000A4 4E75            rts             * routine done
86
87 000000A6 1E25            nzlf:   move.b  -(a5),d7        * get character
88 000000A8 024700FF        andi.w  #$ff,d7         * normal char.
89
90 000000AC 3F07            move.w  d7,-(sp)        * output char
91 000000AE 3F3C0002        move.w  #2,-(sp)        * Code: CONOUT
92 000000B2 4E41            trap    #1              * Call GEMDOS
93 000000B4 588F            addq.l  #4,sp           * Stack correction
94
95 000000B6 60E4            bra     out             * test if done
96
97
98 000000B8 3F3C0000        end:    move.w  #0,-(sp)        * Code WARMSTART
99 000000BC 4E41            trap    #1              * Call GEMDOS
100
101
102 000000BE 3F3C000D       crlf:   move.w  #13,-(sp)       * Output CR
103 000000C2 3F3C0002       move.w  #2,-(sp)        * Code: CONOUT
104 000000C6 4E41           trap    #1              * Call GEMDOS
105 000000C8 588F           addq.l  #4,sp           * Stack correction
106
107 000000CA 3F3C000A       move.w  #10,-(sp)       * Output LF
108 000000CE 3F3C0002       move.w  #2,-(sp)        * Code: CONOUT
109 000000D2 4E41           trap    #1              * Call GEMDOS
110 000000D4 588F           addq.l  #4,sp           * Stack correction
111
112 000000D6 4E75           rts             * Return
113
114
115 000000D8 4287           summ:   clr.l   d7              * Clear sum
116 000000DA 4286           clr.l   d6              * Clear number
117 000000DC                .page
```

235

```
118 000000DC B9FC00000144      sum:   cmpa.l  #tab,a4      * Done?
119 000000E2 6306                     bls     avg          * Y: form average
120
121 000000E4 5286                     addq.l  #1,d6        * incre. counter
122 000000E6 DE64                     add.w   -(a4),d7     * Table value
123
124 000000E8 60F2                     bra     sum          * Next number
125
126 000000EA 8EC6              avg:    divu.w  d6,d7        * average
127
128 000000EC 61D0                     bsr     crlf         * cursor new line
129 000000EE 6100FF7E                 bsr     decout       * output result
130
131 000000F2 60C4                     bra     end          * End program
132
133
134 000000F4              line:   .ds.b 80          * 80 char buffer
135
136 00000144              tab:    .ds.w 100         * 100 values
137
138
139 0000020C                      .end
```

236

The machine code segment that calculates the arithmetic mean is the only new part of this program. The mean is calculated by adding all of the elements and dividing this sum by the number of elements.

A temporary storage area for the elements is not required to calculate the average. The numbers can be counted and summed within the input loop. Despite this fact, we will choose the somewhat more complicated way in order to more clearly illustrate how tables are processed.

In line 8 a pointer is set to the data area TAB which is defined in line 136. Here we will store the values entered word by word. The input loop starts at line 10. Here a subroutine for outputting "CR/LF" is called. This subroutine is defined in lines 102-112. Each input line starts with a prompt ("?") which is created by lines 12 to 15. A decimal number is read in by lines 17 to 26. If a blank line was not entered (lines 28 and 29), the input is converted to register format (in D7). The conversion routine from line 31 to line 55 is one we have used before. The converted number is placed in the table by the instruction in line 58 and the pointer is advanced to the next element. After the word is stored, another number can be entered (line 60).

If a blank line is entered, the program branches from line 29 to line 115. Now the average is actually calculated. The registers for the sum and number of the elements are initialized in lines 115 and 116. The table is processed from last to first element. In lines 118-119 the pointer (A5) is compared to the start of the table as the end criteria, and if the end is reached, a branch is made to line 126.

Otherwise the counter is incremented by one in line 121. Remember that the address register A4 always points to the next element in the table. To

237

sum the elements, we access the element preceding the pointer in line 122. The loop is terminated by an unconditional branch to the top of the loop (line 124). There a check is made to see if all elements have been processed.

If all elements have been summed (in D7) and their number determined (in D6), the average can be calculated by the division in line 126. The result is again placed in D7.

In this example, a decimal number is printed by a subroutine located between lines 63 and 95. The algorithm used is the same as that in the previous examples.

The output of the average value is preceded by a CR/LF in line 128. The result (D7) is then printed by calling the subroutine decout in line 129 and the program is ended in the usual manner (lines 131, 98 and 99).

Simple sorting

With this example we'll explain how to sort a simple table. Large portions of this program correspond to routines which we used for calculating averages.

Decimal numbers are to be entered in an input loop and stored as elements of a table. When the first blank line is entered, the programs starts the sorting procedure and outputs all of the elements in decimal as the result.

For the sorting we use one of the simplest algorithms, a variation of the bubble sort. We have chosen this sorting method because it is easy to understand and to program.

In our sort procedure all of the elements are processed within two loops. The inner loop determines the smallest table element between the nth element and the end of the table. The nth element is always compared with all the others. If a smaller element is found, the two are exchanged. When the loop is done, the smallest of all the elements in the inner loop is in the nth element. The outer loop ensures that the inner loop is executed once for each element. The smallest element in the entire table is found in the first pass through the loop and this is stored at the first position in the table. This process is then repeated for the rest of the table until all elements are sorted.

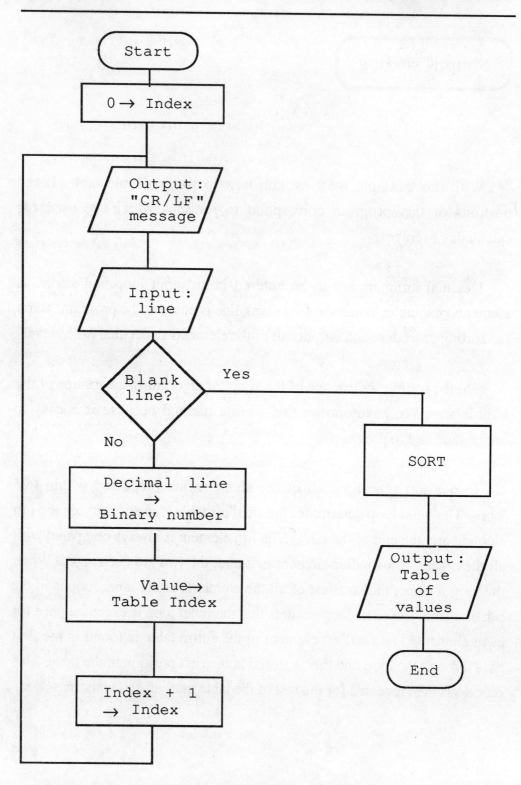

```
C P / M   6 8 0 0 0   A s s e m b l e r          Revision 04.03        Page    1
Source File: B:EXP4.S


 1
 2
 3                                  ********************************************
 4                                  * Simple number sorting         Example 4*
 5                                  ********************************************
 6
 7
 8 00000000 287C00000162            movea.l  #tab,a4        * Data area for #s
 9
10 00000006 610000B6       loop:    bsr      crlf           * Cursor new line
11
12 0000000A 3F3C203F                move.w   #" ?",-(sp)    * Prompt char
13 0000000E 3F3C0002                move.w   #2,-(sp)       * Code: CONOUT
14 00000012 4E41                    trap     #1             * Call GEMDOS
15 00000014 588F                    addq.l   #4,sp          * Stack correction
16
17 00000016 2A7C00000112            movea.l  #line,a5       * Set pointer
18
19 0000001C 3F3C0001       in:      move.w   #1,-(sp)       * Cod: CONIN
20 00000020 4E41                    trap     #1             * Call GEMDOS
21 00000022 548F                    addq.l   #2,sp          * Stack correction
22
23 00000024 1AC0                    move.b   d0,(a5)+       * save character
24
25 00000026 0C00000D                cmpi.b   #13,d0         * char a "CR"?
26 0000002A 66F0                    bne      in             * N: next character
27
28 0000002C BBFC00000113            cmpa.l   #line+1,a5     * Test for blank
29 00000032 670000A4                beq      sort           * Y: sort
30
31 00000036 2A7C00000112            movea.l  #line,a5       * Reset pointer
32
33 0000003C 4287                    clr.l    d7             * clr. result field
34 0000003E 4286                    clr.l    d6             * calc. field(rem)
35
36 00000040 1C1D           convet:  move.b   (a5)+,d6       * process digit
37 00000042 04060030                subi.b   ##30,d6        * ACCII to BCD
38
39 00000046 0C060009                cmpi.b   #9,d6          * BCD digit OK
40 0000004A 621E                    bhi      proces         * Y: no more digit
41 0000004C                .page
```

241

```
42 0000004C CEFC000A              mulu.w  #10,D7         * place shift
43 00000050 DE86                  add.l   d6,d7          * add digit
44
45 00000052 0C870000FFFF          cmpi.l  #$ffff,d7      * test for carry
46 00000058 63E6                  bls     convet         * N: new digit
47
48 0000005A 6162                  bsr     crlf           * cursor new line
49
50 0000005C 3F3C2021              move.w  #" !",-(sp)     * error message
51 00000060 3F3C0002              move.w  #2,-(sp)       * Code CONOUT
52 00000064 4E41                  trap    #1             * Call GEMDOS
53 00000066 588F                  addq.l  #4,sp          * Stack correction
54
55 00000068 609C                  bra     loop           * enter new #
56
57 0000006A 38C7         proces:  move.w  d7,(a4)+       * value in table
58
59 0000006C 6098                  bra     loop           * enter new line
60
61
62
63 0000006E 3F3C203D     decout:  move.w  #" =",-(sp)     * result message
64 00000072 3F3C0002              move.w  #2,-(sp)       * Code: CONOUT
65 00000076 4E41                  trap    #1             * Call GEMDOS
66 00000078 588F                  addq.l  #4,sp          * Stack correction
67
68 0000007A 02870000FFFF          andi.l  #$ffff,d7      * limit places
69
70 00000080 2A7C00000112          movea.l #line,a5       * Set pointer
71
72 00000086 2C07         dodec:   move.l  d7,d6          * process digit
73 00000088 8CFC000A              divu.w  #10,d6         * form value/10
74 0000008C 3E06                  move.w  d6,d7          * save results
75 0000008E 4846                  swap.w  d6             * form remainder
76 00000090 06460030              addi.w  #$30,d6        * generate ASCII
77 00000094 1AC6                  move.b  d6,(a5)+       * digit in buffer
78
79 00000096 0C470000              cmpi.w  #0,d7          * all digits?
80 0000009A 66EA                  bne     dodec          * N; next digit
81 0000009C              .page
```

242

```
 82 0000009C BBFC00000112    out:    cmpa.l  #line,a5        * test buffer
 83 000000A2 6602            bne     nzlf            * N: all digits
 84
 85 000000A4 4E75            rts             * routine done
 86
 87 000000A6 1E25            nzlf:   move.b  -(a5),d7        * get character
 88 000000A8 024700FF        andi.w  #$ff,d7         * normal char.
 89 000000AC 3F07            move.w  d7,-(sp)        * outputf char
 90 000000AE 3F3C0002        move.w  #2,-(sp)        * Code: CONOUT
 91 000000B2 4E41            trap    #1              * Call GEMDOS
 92 000000B4 588F            addq.l  #4,sp           * Stack correction
 93
 94 000000B6 60E4            bra     out             * test if done
 95
 96
 97 000000B8 3F3C0000        end:    move.w  #0,-(sp)        * Code WARMSTART
 98 000000BC 4E41            trap    #1              * Call GEMDOS
 99
100
101 000000BE 3F3C000D        crlf:   move.w  #13,-(sp)       * Output CR
102 000000C2 3F3C0002        move.w  #2,-(sp)        * Code: CONOUT
103 000000C6 4E41            trap    #1              * Call GEMDOS
104 000000C8 588F            addq.l  #4,sp           * Stack correction
105
106 000000CA 3F3C000A        move.w  #10,-(sp)       * Output LF
107 000000CE 3F3C0002        move.w  #2,-(sp)        * Code: CONOUT
108 000000D2 4E41            trap    #1              * Call GEMDOS
109 000000D4 588F            addq.l  #4,sp           * Stack correction
110
111 000000D6 4E75            rts             * Return
112
113
114 000000DB 267C00000162    sort:   movea.l #tab,a3         * 1st index
115
116 000000DE 244B            dosort: movea.l a3,a2           * 2nd index
117 000000E0                 .page
```

```
118 000000E0 3E13          next:    move.w  (a3),d7        # temp register
119 000000E2 3C12                   move.w  (a2),d6        # temp register
120
121 000000E4 BC47                   cmp.w   d7,d6          # test
122 000000E6 6504                   blo     noswap         # Y: no exchange
123
124 000000E8 3487                   move.w  d7,(a2)        # Swap
125 000000EA 3686                   move.w  d6,(a3)
126
127 000000EC D5FC00000002  noswap:  adda.l  #2,a2          # incre. 2nd index
128 000000F2 B5CC                   cmpa.l  a4,a2          # end of table?
129 000000F4 65EA                   blo     next           # Y; continue test
130
131 000000F6 D7FC00000002           adda.l  #2,a3          # incre. 1st index
132 000000FC B7CC                   cmpa.l  a4,a3          # Table done
133 000000FE 65DE                   blo     dosort         # Y; continue sort
134
135 00000100 B9FC00000162  disp:    cmpa.l  #tab,a4        # done
136 00000106 63B0                   bls     end            # Y: end program
137
138 00000108 3E24                   move.w  -(a4),d7       # Table value
139
140 0000010A 61B2                   bsr     crlf           # New line
141 0000010C 6100FF60               bsr     decout         # Output value
142
143 00000110 60EE                   bra     disp           # next
144
145
146
147 00000112          line:    .ds.b 80          # 80 char buffer
148
149 00000162          tab:     .ds.w 100         # 100 values
150
151 0000022A          hip:     .ds.l 1           # temp storage
152
153
154 0000022E                   .end
```

In line 8 a pointer is set to the data area. The data entered will be stored there word by word. The data area is defined in line 149. The input loop starts at line 10. Here a subroutine to output CR/LF is called. The subroutine is defined in lines 101 to 111. Each input line starts with an input prompt ("?") which is created in lines 12 to 15. A decimal number is read in lines 17 through 29. If the line entered is not blank (lines 28 and 29), the input is converted into register format in D7. The conversion routine in lines 31 to 55 is one we have seen before. The converted number is placed in the table by the instruction in line 57. The pointer is also advanced to the next element. After the value is stored, another number can be entered (line 59).

If a blank line is entered, the program branches from line 29 to line 114. Here the actual sorting is done.

The sorting is done in lines 114-133. The inner loop is made up of lines 118 through 129. In line 114 the pointer for the sort loops is set to the first element in the table. In line 116 this is copied as the pointer for the inner loop. In lines 122 to 124 the element from the outer loop is compared with that in the inner and the two are exchanged if requires (lines 124 and 125). The inner loop counter is incremented in lines 127-129, and as long as the last element has not been reached, the loop will be repeated at line 118. If the inner loop is done, the element to which A3 points contains the smallest value. The outer loop is then repeated by the lines in 131 to 133 until all elements have been processed.

The following figure should clarify the sorting procedure.

4 3 2 5 1   Both pointers point to the same element

4 3 2 5 1   Exchange elements

3 4 2 5 1   Exchange elements

2 4 3 5 1   OK, no exchange

2 4 3 5 1   Exchange elements

1 4 3 5 2   Both pointers point to the same element

1 4 3 5 2   Exchange elements

1 3 4 5 2   OK, no exchange

1 3 4 5 2   Exchange elements

1 2 4 5 3   Both pointers point to the same element

1 2 4 5 3   OK, no exchange

1 2 4 5 3   Exchange elements

1 2 3 5 4   Both pointers point to the same element

1 2 3 5 4   Exchange elements

1 2 3 4 5   All elements are sorted

Once all elements are sorted they will be printed in a loop (lines 135 to 143). The output of a decimal number is realized in this example again through a subroutine which is located between lines 63 and 94. The algorithm used is the one we used before.

The output of an element is preceded by the output of a CR/LF in line 140. The element is then printed by a call to the subroutine "decout" in line 141. In this form of output, the largest element is printed first. The loop is closed with the unconditional branch command in line 143. If the comparison in lines 135 and 136 determine that all elements have been printed, the program branches to line 97 where it is ended in the usual manner (lines 136, 97 and 98).

Output: Strings

With this and the following example we want to clarify the use of further operating system subroutines.

By using GEM-DOS function 9, we can output an entire character string on the screen, a string which will be created as a constant in the assembly language program. At the end of the output the program should wait until a key is pressed. Here we can use GEM-DOS function 7. This corresponds to GEM-DOS function 2 except that the character entered is not echoed on the screen. This way you can input even "non-printable" characters (like CTRL-C, etc.) with GEM-DOS function 7.

In line 8 the address of the string to be printed is placed on the stack as a long word. The function code follows in line 9. GEM-DOS is called as usual. The GEM-DOS routine outputs the characters found at the address passed. It ends its activity when it encounters a $00 character. All other codes are permitted, including CR or LF. The stack must be corrected by 6 bytes in line 11 (an account of the long word). Lines 13 to 15 call a special form of console input in which the character entered does not appear on the screen, but is returned in the D0 register. Lines 17 and 18 end the program. Lines 21 and 23 create the text to be printed.

```
 1
 2
 3                          *******************************************
 4                          * Output a string                Example 5*
 5                          *******************************************
 6
 7
 8 00000000 2F3C0000001C    start:   move.L  #text,-(sp)    * Addr. of string
 9 00000006 3F3C0009                 move.w  #9,-(sp)       * Code: PRTLINE
10 0000000A 4E41                     trap    #1             * Call GEMDOS
11 0000000C 5C8F                     addq.l  #6,sp          * Stack correction
12
13 0000000E 3F3C0007                 move.w  #7,-(sp)       * Code: CONIN
14 00000012 4E41                     trap    #1             * Call GEMDOS
15 00000014 548F                     addq.l  #2,sp          * Stack correction
16
17 00000016 3F3C0000                 move.w  #0,-(sp)       * Code: WARMSTART
18 0000001A 4E41                     trap    #1             * Call GEMDOS
19
20
21 0000001C 48656C6C6F2C2077  text:   .dc.b "Hello, world  !!!!!!!!"*
21 00000024 6F726C6420202121
21 0000002C 2121212100
22
23 00000031 0D0A00                   .dc.b 13,10,0    * CR/LF end mark
24
25 00000034                          .end
```

248

Input: String with check

By using GEM-DOS function 9 we can output text on tothe screen. The character string to be printed is defined in the assembly language program. At the conclusion of the output, the program will read a decimal number from the keyboard. Only the number keys and the return key (CR) should be allowed. Here we use GEM-DOS function 7 because with this input function, the character entered does not automatically appear on the screen. We can then first check the validity of the key, and ignore it in case of an error. We must, however, take care of the output of a valid key ourselves. To check to see if the input is correct, we want to output the decimal number once again at the conclusion of the input and end the program.

On the following pages are the flowchart and assembly language program listing.

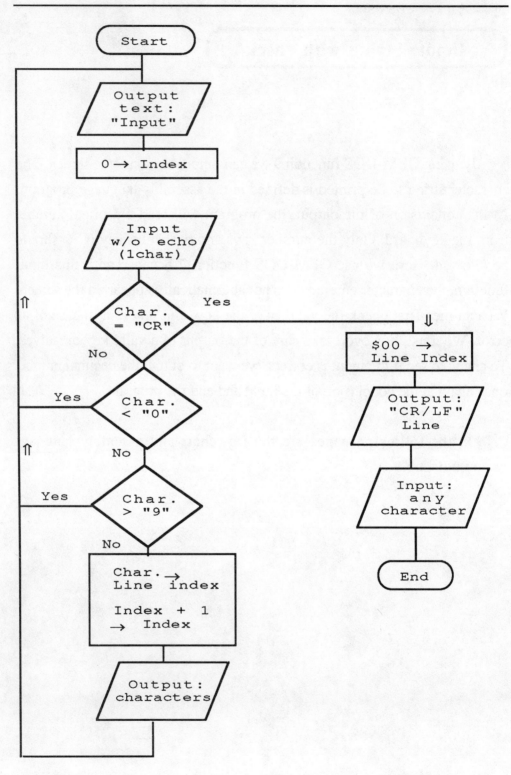

```
C P / M   6 8 0 0 0   A s s e m b l e r        Revision 04.03        Page   1
Source File: B:EXP6.S

 1
 2
 3                              **********************************************
 4                              * Input with check             Example 6*
 5                              **********************************************
 6
 7
 8 00000000 2F3C0000005A       start:  move.l  #text,-(sp)     * Addr. of string
 9 00000006 3F3C0009                   move.w  #9,-(sp)        * Code: PRTLINE
10 0000000A 4E41                       trap    #1              * Call GEMDOS
11 0000000C 5C8F                       addq.l  #6,sp           * Stack correction
12
13 0000000E 2A7C0000006B               move.l  #texbuf,a5      * Pointer to text buf
14
15 00000014 3F3C0007         in:       move.w  #7,-(sp)        * Code: CONIN
16 00000018 4E41                       trap    #1              * Call GEMDOS
17 0000001A 548F                       addq.l  #2,sp           * Stack correction
18
19 0000001C 0C00000D                   cmpi.b  #$0d,d0         * char a CR?
20 00000020 671A                       beq     out             * Y; output line
21
22 00000022 0C000039                   cmpi.b  #$39,d0         * char > 9?
23 00000026 62EC                       bhi     in              * Y; ingore
24
25 00000028 0C000030                   cmpi.b  #$30,d0         * char < 0?
26 0000002C 65E6                       blo     in              * Y; ingore
27
28 0000002E 1AC0                       move.b  d0,(a5)+        * store char.
29
30 00000030 3F00                       move.w  d0,-(sp)        * output char
31 00000032 3F3C0002                   move.w  #2,-(sp)        * Code: CONOUT
32 00000036 4E41                       trap    #1              * Call GEMDOS
33 00000038 588F                       addq.l  #4,sp           * Stack correction
34
35 0000003A 60D8                       bra     in              * next character
36
37 0000003C                  .page
```

251

```
C P / M   6 8 0 0 0   A s s e m b l e r          Revision 04.03        Page  2
Source File: B:EXP6.S


38 0000003C 4215              out:    clr.b   (a5)              * mark end of line
39
40 0000003E 2F3C00000066              move.l  #outbuf,-(sp)     *addr. of buff
41 00000044 3F3C0009                  move.w  #9,-(sp)          * Code: PRTLINE
42 00000048 4E41                      trap    #1                * Call GEMDOS
43 0000004A 5C8F                      addq.l  #6,sp             * Stack correction
44
45 0000004C 3F3C0007                  move.w  #7,-(sp)          * Code: CONIN
46 00000050 4E41                      trap    #1                * Call GEMDOS
47 00000052 548F                      addq.l  #2,sp             * Stack correction
48
49 00000054 3F3C0000                  move.w  #0,-(sp)          * Code: WARMSTART
50 00000058 4E41                      trap    #1                * Call GEMDOS
51
52
53 0000005A 0D0A496E70757420 text:    .dc.b   $0D,$0A,"Input  #:",$0
53 00000062 20233A00
54
55 00000066 0D0A             outbuf: .dc.b   $0d,$0a
56
57 00000068             texbuf: .ds.b   40
58
59
60 00000090                          .end
```

Lines 8 to 11 output the initial text on the screen ; in line 13 the input buffer pointer is set up. Lines 15 to 17 read a character, but without displaying it on the screen. If the character was a CR, the input is terminated and the input buffer is printed at line 38.

Lines 22 to 26 check to see if the character entered is valid. If not, the program branches to the top of the input loop (line 15). Only if the character is valid is it placed in the input buffer and the pointer incremented (line 28). The valid character must then be printed on the screen so that the user sees that the input was accepted (lines 30 to 33). Once this is done, execution branches back to the top of the input loop (line 35).

The decimal number in the input buffer is printed by the code starting in line 38. Here we again use the output function for a whole character string. But first we must mark the end of the input buffer with a $00 (line 38). Note that for the output (lines 40 to 43) we do not specify the address of the input buffer, but that of the output buffer (lines 55 and 57). Here we use a simple trick to output another CR/LF before the actual output. If you look at the declarations at line 53, you will see that the output buffer and the input buffer overlap, because the output buffer is not marked with a $00 to indicate its end.

Another keyboard input is expected in lines 45 to 47 before the instructions in lines 49 and 50 are executed to end the program.

Output: Date

With this example we want to illustrate GEM-DOS function 42, which allows you to use the date (month, day, year) in your programs.

The program in our example should simply read the current date and display it in the form MM/DD/YY in decimal on the screen. Here we use our old subroutine for outputting a decimal number and for creating a linefeed.

First we will briefly explain how the date is read. After calling the DATE function, GEM-DOS returns the date coded in binary in the D0 register. The bits have the following significance:

Bits 0 to 4	**day**	Range: binary 1 to 31
Bits 5 to 8	**month**	Range: binary 1 to 12
Bits 9 to 15	**year**	Range: binary 0 to 119

The year refers to the years since 1980. In order to get the correct year value, the constant 1980 must be added to the year field.

The following pages contain the program flowchart and the assembly language program listing.

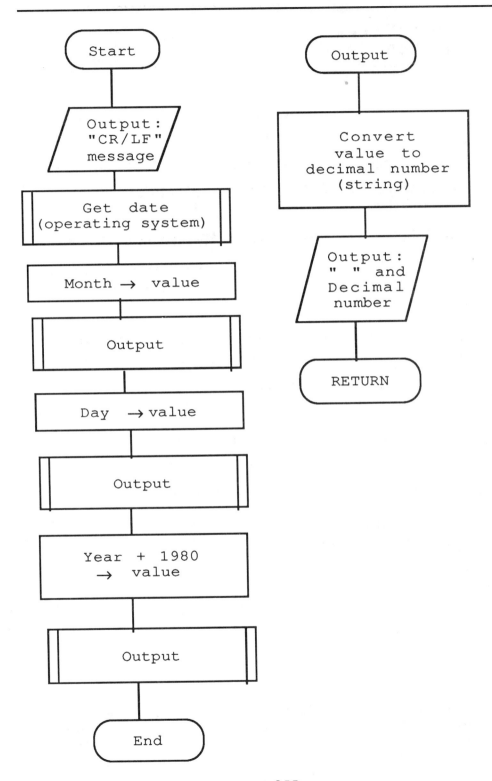

```
C P / M   6 8 0 0 0   A s s e m b l e r         Revision 04.03        Page  1
Source File: B:EXP7.S


   1
   2
   3                              ***********************************************
   4                              * OUTPUT DATE                      Example 7*
   5                              ***********************************************
   6
   7
   8 00000000 61000094                      jsr    crlf          * Cursor new line
   9
  10 00000004 3F3C002A                      move.w #$2a,-(sp)    * Code: GETDATE
  11 00000008 4E41                          trap   #1            * Call GEMDOS
  12 0000000A 548F                          addq.l #2,sp         * Stack correction
  13
  14 0000000C 33C000000100                  move.w d0,hip        * Save date
  15
  16 00000012 02B00000001E0                 andi.l #$1e0,d0      * process month
  17 00000018 EA88                          lsr.l  #5,d0
  18 0000001A 2E00                          move.l d0,d7         * prepare output
  19
  20 0000001C 6128                          bsr    decout        * and output
  21
  22 0000001E 3E3900000100                  move.w hip,d7        * Get data
  23
  24 00000024 02870000001F                  andi.l #$1f,d7       * isolate day
  25 0000002A 611A                          bsr    decout        * and output
  26
  27 0000002C 3E3900000100                  move.w hip,d7        * Get data
  28
  29 00000032 02B00000FE00                  andi.l #$fe00,d0     * isolate year
  30 00000038 7C09                          move.l #9,d6         * set number shift
  31 0000003A ECAF                          lsr.l  d6,d7         * and norm (9x)
  32 0000003C 0687000007BC                  addi.l #1980,d7      * constant 1980
  33 00000042 6102                          bsr    decout        * and output
  34
  35 00000044 604A                          bra    end           * end program
  36
  37
  38 00000046 3F3C2020      decout: move.w #" ",-(sp)    * space as seperator
  39 0000004A 3F3C0002              move.w #2,-(sp)      * Code: CONOUT
  40 0000004E 4E41                  trap   #1            * Call GEMDOS
  41 00000050 588F                  addq.l #4,sp         * Stack correction
  42 00000052                .page
```

256

```
CP/M 68000 Assembler            Revision 04.03        Page   2
Source File: B:EXP7.S

 43 00000052 02870000FFFF              andi.l   #$ffff,d7      * limit places
 44
 45 00000058 2A7C000000B0              movea.l  #line,a5       * Set pointer
 46
 47 0000005E 2C07          dodec:      move.l   d7,d6          * process digit
 48 00000060 8CFC000A                  divu.w   #10,d6         * form value/10
 49 00000064 3E06                      move.w   d6,d7          * save results
 50 00000066 4846                      swap.w   d6             * form remainder
 51 00000068 06460030                  addi.w   #$30,d6        * generate ASCII
 52 0000006C 1AC6                      move.b   d6,(a5)+       * in buffer
 53
 54 0000006E 0C470000                  cmpi.w   #0,d7          * all digits?
 55 00000072 66EA                      bne      dodec          * N; next digit
 56
 57 00000074 BBFC000000B0  out:        cmpa.l   #line,a5       * test buffer
 58 0000007A 6602                      bne      nzlf           * N: all digits
 59
 60 0000007C 4E75                      rts                     * routine done
 61
 62 0000007E 1E25          nzlf:       move.b   -(a5),d7       * get character
 63 00000080 024700FF                  andi.w   #$ff,d7        * normal char.
 64
 65 00000084 3F07                      move.w   d7,-(sp)       * output char
 66 00000086 3F3C0002                  move.w   #2,-(sp)       * Code: CONOUT
 67 0000008A 4E41                      trap     #1             * Call GEMDOS
 68 0000008C 588F                      addq.l   #4,sp          * Stack correction
 69
 70 0000008E 60E4                      bra      out            * test if done
 71
 72
 73 00000090 3F3C0000      end:        move.w   #0,-(sp)       * Code WARMSTART
 74 00000094 4E41                      trap     #1             * Call GEMDOS
 75
 76
 77 00000096 3F3C000D      crlf:       move.w   #13,-(sp)      * Output CR
 78 0000009A 3F3C0002                  move.w   #2,-(sp)       * Code: CONOUT
 79 0000009E 4E41                      trap     #1             * Call GEMDOS
 80 000000A0 588F                      addq.l   #4,sp          * Stack correction
 81 000000A2                           .page
```

```
82 000000A2 3F3C000A          move.w  #10,-(sp)      * Output LF
83 000000A6 3F3C0002          move.w  #2,-(sp)       * Code: CONOUT
84 000000AA 4E41              trap    #1             * Call GEMDOS
85 000000AC 588F              addq.l  #4,sp          * Stack correction
86
87 000000AE 4E75              rts                    * Return
88
89
90 000000B0          line:    .ds.b 80               * 80 char buffer
91
92 00000100          hip:     .ds.l 1                * Date temp. store
93
94 00000104                   .end
```

The routines to output a decimal number (lines 38 to 70) and the subroutine for CR/LF (lines 77 to 87) are familiar to us already. The output of the date stretches from line 8 to line 35.

First a CR/LF is output and the GEM-DOS function for reading the date is called (lines 8-12). The date in D0 is saved before it is processed (line 14). The day is printed in lines 16 to 19. The day is formed through simple masking (line 16). Outputting the month is just as simple (lines 21 to 25), only the result must be shifted right to put it in the right part of the word after the rest of the number is masked out in line 23. The month is then printed (line 25).

Forming the year is somewhat more complicated. After the other parts of the data are masked out in line 29, the number must averaged through multiple right-shifts (lines 30 and 31) since a shift cannot move a value more than 7 bits at a time. After this we add the constant 1980 in line 32 in order to get the correct the year. Lines 35, 73, and 64 end the program in the usual manner.

Factorial calculation

The factorial of n (where n is an integer) is defined as the product of the first n natural numbers:

n! = 1 * 2 * 3 * ... * n,   where 0! is defined to be 1.

Examples:

```
0! = 1     =   1
1! = 1*0! =   1
2! = 2*1! =   2
3! = 3*2! =   6
4! = 4*3! =  24     (etc.)
```

Clearly, we can also define the factorial of the number "n" in a different manner:

0! = 1   and   n! = (n-1)!

This form of the definition is called **recursive**. Each following element can be determined through its predecessors, and has great application in computer science. We speak of a recursive program (in contrast to iterative) if a routine calls *itself* directly or indirectly. Naturally you must ensure that this cycle of self-calls ends at some point.

Recursive representations have the advantage of being proven relatively easily. We will not calculate a factorial iteratively, because it represents a relatively simple example of recursion—although it is still the most difficult concept presented in this book.

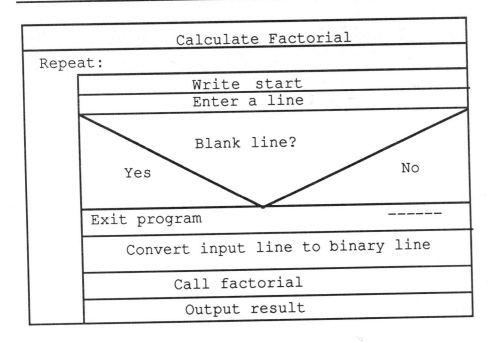

```
┌─────────────────────────────────────────────────┐
│              Calculate Factorial                │
├─────────────────────────────────────────────────┤
│ Repeat:                                         │
│      ┌──────────────────────────────────────┐   │
│      │           Write  start               │   │
│      ├──────────────────────────────────────┤   │
│      │           Enter a line               │   │
│      ├──────────────────────────────────────┤   │
│      │ \            Blank line?          /  │   │
│      │   \                            /     │   │
│      │  Yes \                      / No      │   │
│      ├──────────────────────────────────────┤   │
│      │ Exit program          ------         │   │
│      ├──────────────────────────────────────┤   │
│      │  Convert input line to binary line   │   │
│      ├──────────────────────────────────────┤   │
│      │           Call factorial             │   │
│      ├──────────────────────────────────────┤   │
│      │           Output result              │   │
│      └──────────────────────────────────────┘   │
└─────────────────────────────────────────────────┘
```

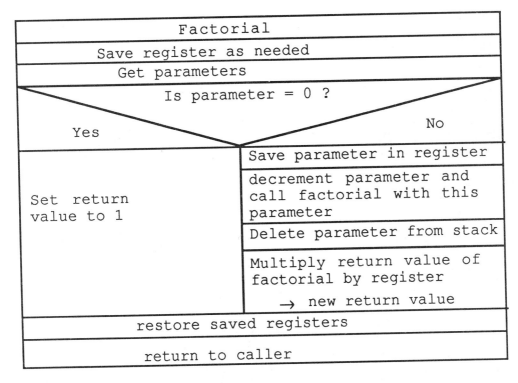

```
┌─────────────────────────────────────────────────┐
│                  Factorial                      │
├─────────────────────────────────────────────────┤
│          Save register as needed                │
├─────────────────────────────────────────────────┤
│              Get parameters                     │
├─────────────────────────────────────────────────┤
│ \            Is parameter = 0 ?             /   │
│   \                                      /      │
│ Yes \                              No  /        │
├───────────────┬─────────────────────────────────┤
│               │ Save parameter in register      │
│               ├─────────────────────────────────┤
│               │ decrement parameter and         │
│ Set  return   │ call factorial with this        │
│ value to 1    │ parameter                       │
│               ├─────────────────────────────────┤
│               │ Delete parameter from stack     │
│               ├─────────────────────────────────┤
│               │ Multiply return value of        │
│               │ factorial by register           │
│               │    → new return value           │
├───────────────┴─────────────────────────────────┤
│            restore saved registers              │
├─────────────────────────────────────────────────┤
│              return to caller                   │
└─────────────────────────────────────────────────┘
```

```
    1
    2
    3                                 ************************************************
    4                                 * CALCULATE FACTORIal                Example 8*
    5                                 ************************************************
    6
    7
    8 00000000 610000E6       loop:   bsr     crlf            * Cursor new line
    9
   10 00000004 3F3C203F               move.w  #" ?",-(sp)     * Prompt char
   11 00000008 3F3C0002               move.w  #2,-(sp)        * Code: CONOUT
   12 0000000C 4E41                   trap    #1              * Call GEMDOS
   13 0000000E 588F                   addq.l  #4,sp           * Stack correction
   14
   15 00000010 2A7C00000102           movea.l #line,a5        * Set pointer
   16
   17 00000016 3F3C0001       in:     move.w  #1,-(sp)        * Cod: CONIN
   18 0000001A 4E41                   trap    #1              * Call GEMDOS
   19 0000001C 1AC0                   move.b  d0,(a5)+        * store char
   20 0000001E 548F                   addq.l  #2,sp           * Stack correction
   21
   22 00000020 0C00000D               cmpi.b  #13,d0          * char a "CR"?
   23 00000024 66F0                   bne     in              *N: next character
   24
   25 00000026 BBFC00000103           cmpa.l  #line+1,a5      * Test for blank
   26 0000002C 670000B4               beq     end             * Y:end program
   27
   28 00000030 2A7C00000102           movea.l #line,a5        * Reset pointer
   29
   30 00000036 4287                   clr.l   d7              *clr. result field
   31 00000038 4286                   clr.l   d6              * calc. field(remainder)
   32
   33 0000003A 1C1D           convet: move.b  (a5)+,d6        * process digit
   34 0000003C 04060030               subi.b  #$30,d6         * ACCII to BCD
   35
   36 00000040 0C060009               cmpi.b  #9,d6           * BCD digit OK
   37 00000044 6220                   bhi     proces          * Y: no more digit
   38
   39 00000046 CEFC000A               mulu.w  #10,D7          * place shift
   40 0000004A DE86                   add.l   d6,d7           * add digit
   41 0000004C                .page
```

```
42 0000004C 0C870000FFFF          cmpi.l  #$ffff,d7        * test for carry
43 00000052 63E6                  bls     convet           * N: new digit
44
45 00000054 61000092              bsr     crlf             * cursor new line
46
47 00000058 3F3C2021              move.w  #" !",-(sp)       * error message
48 0000005C 3F3C0002              move.w  #2,-(sp)          * Code CONOUT
49 00000060 4E41                  trap    #1               * Call GEMDOS
50 00000062 588F                  addq.l  #4,sp            * Stack correction
51
52 00000064 609A                  bra     loop             * enter new #
53
54
55 00000066 2F07          proces: move.l  d7,-(sp)         * factorial
56 00000068 6104                  bsr     fac              * calculate
57 0000006A 588F                  addq.l  #4,sp            * param,from stack
58 0000006C 6028                  bra     decout           * and output
59
60
61 0000006E 4E540000      fac:    link    a4,#0            * local stack
62 00000072 2F05                  move.l  d5,-(sp)          * save register
63 00000074 2A2C0008              move.l  8(a4),d5          * get parameter
64 00000078 0C8500000000          cmpi.l  #0,d5            * check end
65 0000007E 6712                  beq     endfac           * Y: done
66 00000080 2C05                  move.l  d5,d6            *copy for dec.
67 00000082 5386                  subq.l  #1,d6            * dec. counter
68 00000084 2F06                  move.l  d6,-(sp)          * new parameter
69 00000086 61E6                  bsr     fac              * recursion
70 00000088 588F                  addq.l  #4,sp            * param. from stack
71 0000008A CEC5                  mulu.w  d5,d7            * calc. n-1
72
73 0000008C 2A1F          savfac: move.l  (sp)+,d5         * remove frm stack
74 0000008E 4E5C                  unlk    a4               * rerlease stack
75 00000090 4E75                  rts                      * rec. level done
76
77 00000092 7E01          endfac: move.l  #1,d7            * recursion done
78 00000094 60F6                  bra     savfac           *end processing
79 00000096               .page
```

```
80
81
82 00000096 6150             decout: bsr      crlf            *cursor new line
83
84 00000098 3F3C203D                 move.w   #" =",-(sp)     * result message
85 0000009C 3F3C0002                 move.w   #2,-(sp)        * Code: CONOUT
86 000000A0 4E41                     trap     #1              * Call GEMDOS
87 000000A2 588F                     addq.l   #4,sp           * Stack correction
88
89 000000A4 02870000FFFF             andi.l   #$ffff,d7       * limit places
90 000000AA 2A7C00000102             movea.l  #line,a5        * Set pointer
91
92 000000B0 2C07             dodec:  move.l   d7,d6           * process digit
93 000000B2 8CFC000A                 divu.w   #10,d6          * form value/10
94 000000B6 3E06                     move.w   d6,d7           * save results
95 000000B8 4846                     swap     d6              * form remainder
96 000000BA 06460030                 addi.w   #$30,d6         *generate ASCII
97 000000BE 1AC6                     move.b   d6,(a5)+        * digit in buffer
98 000000C0 0C470000                 cmpi.w   #0,d7           * all digits
99 000000C4 66EA                     bne      dodec           * N; next digit
100
101 000000C6 BBFC00000102    out:    cmpa.l   #line,a5        * test buffer
102 000000CC 6700FF32                beq      loop            * Y: all digits
103
104 000000D0 1E25                    move.b   -(a5),d7        * get character
105 000000D2 024700FF                andi.w   #$ff,d7         * normal char.
106
107 000000D6 3F07                    move.w   d7,-(sp)        * output char
108 000000D8 3F3C0002                move.w   #2,-(sp)        * Code: CONOUT
109 000000DC 4E41                    trap     #1              * Call GEMDOS
110 000000DE 588F                    addq.l   #4,sp           * Stack correction
111
112 000000E0 60E4                    bra      out             * test if done
113
114
115 000000E2 3F3C0000        end:    move.w   #0,-(sp)        * Code WARMSTART
116 000000E6 4E41                    trap     #1              * Call GEMDOS
117
118 000000E8                 .page
```

```
119 000000E8 3F3C000D      crlf:   move.w  #13,-(sp)      * Output CR
120 000000EC 3F3C0002              move.w  #2,-(sp)       * Code: CONOUT
121 000000F0 4E41                  trap    #1             * Call GEMDOS
122 000000F2 588F                  addq.l  #4,sp          * Stack correction
123
124 000000F4 3F3C000A              move.w  #10,-(sp)      * Output LF
125 000000F8 3F3C0002              move.w  #2,-(sp)       * Code: CONOUT
126 000000FC 4E41                  trap    #1             * Call GEMDOS
127 000000FE 588F                  addq.l  #4,sp          * Stack correction
128
129 00000100 4E75                  rts                    * Return
130
131
132 00000102               line:   .ds.b 80               * 80 char buffer
133
134
135 00000152                       .end
```

This example contains four elements used in previous examples. Only the factorial calculation is new.

The subroutine for output of CR/LF, defined in lines 119 to 129, is called in line 8. Each input line starts with an input prompt ("?") created in lines 10-13. A decimal number is read in by lines 15 to 23. If a blank line was not entered (lines 25 and 26), the input is converted to a binary number. The conversion routine from line 28 to line 52 is one we have used before. The converted number is (line 55) passed to the factorial routine via the stack. After the factorial calculation the stack will be corrected, the result printed in decimal (lines 82 to 112), and new data is requested (line 8).

If a blank line is entered, the program branches from line 26 to line 115. Here the program ends with a jump back to GEM. The actual factorial calculation is performed in lines 61 to 78.

Then a so-called local base is established with the LINK instruction. Several operations are performed when this instruction is executed. First the contents of the A4 register are placed on the stack; then the current stack pointer value is copied into the address register just saved (A4); and the stack pointer is changed by the value given as the destination operand.

If a negative offset is given, the stack pointer is moved down. This creates a "local" address space within the stack area. We do not need any local stack space for the factorial calculation, so we specified a #0 in the LINK instruction.

We use the LINK/UNLK mechanism here in order to simplify the stack management.

The current parameter, found in D5, is saved by the MOVE instruction in line 62. In line 63, the last argument of the factorial function is read from the stack over the local base. If 0 is given as the argument, if the last recursion level is reached, the recursion can be resolved in reverse order (jump to line 77).

If the last recursion level is not reached, the argument decremented by one is pushed on the stack as the new argument by the instructions in lines 66 to 68, and the factorial is called again. If the last recursion level is reached, we have the stack picture (for calculation of 2!) illustrated on the following page.

The recursion is then resolved and the stack is reconstructed, in which a "1" (0!=1) is passed as the function value in D7 back to the calling location as the result of the last recursion level (lines 77 and 78). The stack is constructed at line 73, in which the argument of the caller is restored in D5 and the local stack is released through UNLK. The function is ended by RTS.

The result in D7 will by multiplied by the argument and the stack corrected for as long as the function had called itself (lines 70 and 71).

Higher	Argument "2"	Address "n"
Address		Address "n+2"
	Return address to caller	Address "n+4"
L		
E		
V 1	A4 (save as local base)	Local base 1
E		
L	Data register D5	
	Argument "1"	
L		
E	return address	
V 2		
E	A4 (save as local base)	Local base 2
L		
	with contents "2"	
L	Argument "0"	
E		
V 3	return address	
E		
L	.A4 (save as local base)	Local base 3
Lower		
Address	D5 with contents "1"	User stack pointer

At the conclusion of this chapter, we have one small practice suggestion to recommend: play with the processor yourself! You can duplicate the example of the factorial calculation with paper and pencil. Draw a stack picture showing how the factorial calculation reconstructs the stack, and create a list showing how the values in the registers change. This is not only interesting to observe—it will also deepen your understanding of the last example.

APPENDIX

Flowchart Symbols

Program flowchart:

General processiong:

Branch:

Subroutine:

Input/Output:

Start/End:

Transfer/Continuation:

Condition Codes

Abbreviations for testing the condition codes:

CC	if carry clear	if C=0
CS	if carry set	if C=1
PL	if plus	if N=0
MI	if minus	if N=1
VC	if overflow clear	if V=0
VS	if overflow set	if V=1
NE	if not equal	if Z=0
EQ	if equal	if Z=1

After comparison:

EQ	if equal	if OP1 = OP2
NE	if not equal	if OP1 ≠ OP2

After comparing unsigned values:

LO	if lower	if OP2 < OP1
LS	if lower or same	if OP2 ≤ OP1
HI	if higher	if OP2 > OP1
HS	if higher or same	if OP2 ≥ OP1

After comparing signed values:

LT	less than	if OP2 < OP1
LE	less than or equal	if OP2 ≤ OP1
GT	greater than	if OP2 > OP1
GE	greater than or equal	if OP2 ≥ OP1

Additional:

T	True: The condition is always fulfilled
F	False: The condition is never fulfilled

68000 ADDRESSING MODES

No.	Description	Syntax	Example
1)	Data register direct	Dn	D3
2)	Address register direct	An	A3
3)	Address register indirect	(An)	(A3)
4)	Address register indirect with postincrement	(An)+	(A5)+ (SP)+
5)	Address register indirect with predecrement	-(An)	-(A5) -(SP)
6)	Address register indirect with 16-bit distance value	$d_{16}(An)$	$1234(A5)
7)	Address register indirect with 8-bit distance value	$d_8(An,Rn)$	$C0(A1,D1)
8)	Absolute short	$xxxx.W	$3000
9)	Absolute long	$x..x.L	$12345678
10)	Immediate	#"data"	#$0d
11)	Program counter indirect with 16-bit distance value	$d_{16}(PC)$	$1000(PC)
12)	Program counter indirect with 8-bit distance and index (register)	$d_8(PC)$	$1000(PC)

Rn: any data or address register
Dn: any data register
An: any address register

Instruction Overview

Mnemonic	Function	OP#	1	2	3	4	5	6	7	8	9	10	11	12	XNZVC
					Valid addressing modes										FLAGS
ABCD.X	Add BCD with extend	2	x				x								*u*u*
ADD.X	Add binary	2	s	s	x	x	x	x	x	x	x	s	s	s	*****
ADD.W/L	Add binary to address reg	2	x	x	x	x	x	x	x	x	x	x	x	x	-----
ADDI.X	Add immediate	2	x		x	x	x	x	x	x					*****
ADDQ.X	Add immediate quick	2	x	x	x	x	x	x	x	x					*****
ADDX.X	Add binary with extend	2	x				x								*****
AND.X	Logical AND	2	s		x	x	x	x	x	x	x	s	s	s	-**00
ANDI.X	Logical AND immediate	2	x		x	x	x	x	x	x					-**00
ASL,ASR.X	Arith. shift left/right	1/2	x		x	x	x	x	x	x					*****
Bcc	Branch conditional	1													-----
BCHG.X	Test bit and change	2	x		x	x	x	x	x	x					--*--
BCLR.X	Clear bit	2	x		x	x	x	x	x	x					--*--
BRA	Branch always	1													-----
BSET.X	Bit TEST and SET	2	x		x	x	x	x	x	x					--*--
BSR	Branch to subroutine	1													-----
BTST.X	Bit TEST	2	x		x	x	x	x	x	x					
CHK.W	Check reg against bounds	2	x		x	x	x	x	x	x	x	x			*-UUU
CLR.X	Clear	1	x		x	x	x	x	x	x					-0100
CMP.X	Compare	2	x	x	x	x	x	x	x	x	x	x	x	x	-****
CMPA.X	Compare address register	2	x	x	x	x	x	x	x	x	x	x	x	x	-****
CMPI.X	Compare immediate	2	x		x	x	x	x	x	x					-****
CMPM.X	Compare with memory	2			x			x	x	x	x		x	x	-****
DBcc.W	Decrement and branch	2													-----
DIVS.W	Divide signed	2	x		x	x	x	x	x	x	x	x	x	x	-***0
DIVU.W	Divide unsigned	2	x		x	x	x	x	x	x	x	x	x	x	-***0
EOR.X	Logical exclusive OR	2	x		x	x	x	x	x	x					-**00
EORI.X	EOR immediate	2	x		x	x	x	x	x	x					-**00
EXG.L	Exchange registers	2	x	x											-----
EXT.X	Sign extend	2	x												-**00
JMP	Jump absolute	1			x			x	x	x	x		x	x	-----
JSR	Jump to subroutine	1			x			x	x	x	x		x	x	-----
LEA.L	Load Effective Address	2			x			x	x	x	x		x	x	-----
LINK	Link local base pointer	2		x											-----
LSL,LSR.X	Logical shift left/right	1/2	x		x	x	x	x	x	x					***0*
MOVE.X	Move	2	x	s	x	x	x	x	x	x	x	s	s	s	-**00
MOVEA.W/L	Move to address register	2	x	x	x	x	x	x	x	x	x	x	x	x	-----
MOVE.X	Move to CCR	1	x		x	x	x	x	x	x	x	x	x	x	*****
MOVE.X	Move from SR	1	x		x	x	x	x	x	x					-----
MOVE.X	Move to SR	1	x		x	x	x	x	x	x	x	x	x	x	*****
MOVE.X	Move user stack pointer	1		x											-----
MOVEM.X	Move multiple registers	2			x	s	d	x	x	x	x		s	s	-----

			Valid addressing modes												FLAGS
Mnemonic	Function	OP#	1	2	3	4	5	6	7	8	9	10	11	12	XNZVC
MOVEP.W/L	Move peripheral	2	x					x							-----
MOVEQ.L	Move immediate quick	1	d												-**00
MULS.W	Multiply signed	2	x		x	x	x	x	x	x	x	x	x	x	-**00
MULU.W	Multiply unsigned	2	x		x	x	x	x	x	x	x	x	x	x	-**00
NBCD.B	Negate BCD byte	1	x		x	x	x	x	x	x	x				*U*U*
NEG.X	Negate	1	x		x	x	x	x	x	x	x				*****
NEGX.X	Negate with extend	1	x		x	x	x	x	x	x	x				*****
NOP	No operation	-													-----
NOT.X	Logical NOT	1	x		x	x	x	x	x	x	x				-**00
OR.X	Logical OR	2	x		x	x	x	x	x	x	x	s	s	s	-**00
ORI.X	Logical OR immediate	2	x		x	x	x	x	x	x	x				-**00
PEA.L	Push effective address	1			x			x	x	x	x		x	x	-----
RESET	Reset	-													-----
ROL,ROR.X	Rotate left/right	1/2	x		x	x	x	x	x	x	x				-**0*
ROXL,ROXR.X	Rotate L/R with extend	1/2	x		x	x	x	x	x	x	x				***0*
RTE	Return from exception	-													*****
RTR	Return and restore CCR	-													*****
RTS	Return from subroutine	-													-----
SBCD.B	Subtract BCD with extend	2	x				x								*U*U*
Scc.B	Set byte according to cc	1	x		x	x	x	x	x	x	x				-----
STOP.X	Stop with CCR loaded	1										x			*****
SUB.X	Subtract binary	2	s	s	x	x	x	x	x	x	x	s	s	s	*****
SUBA.W/L	Subt. bin from addr reg	2	x	x	x	x	x	x	x	x	x	x	x	x	-----
SUBI.X	Subtract immediate	2	x		x	x	x	x	x	x	x				*****
SUBQ.X	Subtract quick	2	x	x	x	x	x	x	x	x	x				*****
SUBX.X	Subtract with extend	2	x				x								*****
SWAP	Swap register halves	1	x												-**00
TAS.B	Test byte and SET	1	x		x	x	x	x	x	x	x				-**00
TRAP	Trap	1										x			-----
TRAPV	Trap on overflow	-													-----
TST.X	Test byte	1	x		x	x	x	x	x	x	x				-**00
UNLK	Unlink local area	1		x											-----

Optional Diskette

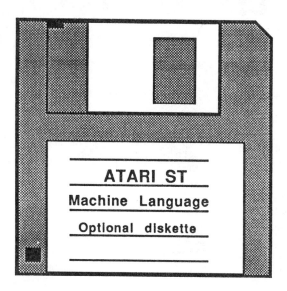

For your convenience, the program listings contained in this book are available on an SF354 formatted floppy disk. You should order the diskette if you want to use the programs, but don't want to type them in from the listings in the book.

All programs on the diskette have been fully tested. You can change the programs for your particular needs. The diskette is available for $14.95 plus $2.00 ($5.00 foreign) for postage and handling.

When ordering, please give your name and shipping address. Enclose a check, money order or credit card information. Mail your order to:

Abacus Software
5370 52nd Street SE
Grand Rapids, MI 49508

Or for fast service, call **616/698-0330**.
Credit Card orders only **1-800-451-4319**.

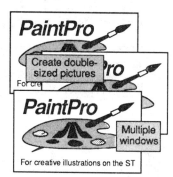
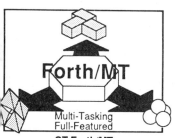

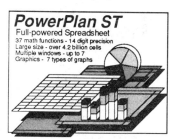

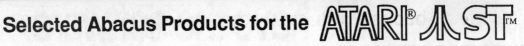
DataRetrieve

(formerly FilePro ST)

Database management package
for the Atari ST

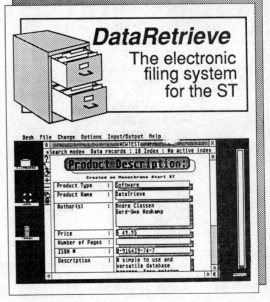

"DataRetrieve is the most versatile, and yet simple, data base manager available for the Atari 520ST/1040ST on the market to date."

—Bruce Mittleman
Atari Journal

DataRetrieve is one of Abacus' best-selling software packages for the Atari ST computers—it's received highest ratings from many leading computer magazines. **DataRetrieve** is perfect for your customers who need a powerful, yet easy to use database system at a moderate price of $49.95.

DataRetrieve's drop-down menus let the user quickly and easily define a file and enter information through screen templates. But even though it's easy to use, **DataRetrieve** is also powerful. **DataRetrieve** has fast search and sorting capabilities, a capacity of up to 64,000 records, and allows numeric values with up to 15 significant digits. **DataRetrieve** lets the user access data from up to four files simultaneously, indexes up to 20 different fields per file, supports multiple files, and has an integral editor for complete reporting capabilities.

DataRetrieve's screen templates are paintable for enhanced appearance on the screen and when printed, and data items may be displayed in multiple type styles and font sizes.

The package includes six predefined databases for mailing list, record/video albums, stamp and coin collection, recipes, home inventory and auto maintenance that users can customize to their own requirements. The templates may be printed on Rolodex cards, as well as 3 x 5 and 4 x 5 index cards. **DataRetrieve's** built-in RAM disks support lightning-fast operation on the 1040ST. **DataRetrieve** interfaces to **TextPro** files, features easy printer control, many help screens, and a complete manual.

DataRetrieve works with Atari ST systems with one or more single- or double-sided disk drives. Works with either monochrome or color monitors. Printer optional.

DataRetrieve   Suggested Retail Price: **$49.95**

DataRetrieve Features:

- Easily define your files using drop-down menus
- Design screen mask size to 5000 by 5000 pixels
- Choose from six font sizes and six text styles
- Add circles, boxes and lines to screen masks
- Fast search and sort capabilities
- Handles records up to 64,000 characters in length
- Organize files with up to 20 indexes
- Access up to four files simultaneously
- Cut, past and copy data to other files
- Change file definitions and format
- Create subsets of files
- Interfaces with **TextPro** files
- Complete built-in reporting capabilities
- Change setup to support virtually any printer
- Add header, footer and page number to reports
- Define printer masks for all reporting needs
- Send output to screen, printer, disk or modem
- Includes and supports RAM disk for high-speed 1040ST operation
- Capacities: max. 2 billion characters per file
  max. 64,000 records per file
  max. 64,000 characters per record
  max. fields: limited only by record size
  max. 32,000 text characters per field
  max. 20 index fields per file
- Index precision: 3 to 20 characters
- Numeric precision: to 15 digits
- Numeric range $\pm 10^{-308}$ ti $\pm 10^{308}$

TextPro

Wordprocessing package for the Atari ST

"TextPro seems to be well thought out, easy, flexible anf fast. The program makes excellent use of the GEM interface and provides lots of small enhancements to make your work go more easily... if you have an ST and haven't moved up to a GEM word processor, pick up this one and become a text pro."

—John Kintz
ANTIC

"TextPro is the best wordprocessor available for the ST"
—Randy McSorley
Pacus Report

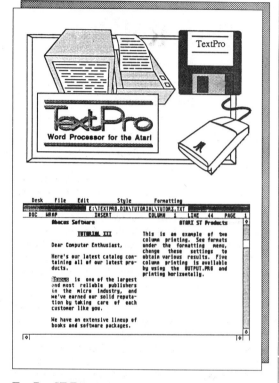

TextPro is a first-class word processor for the Atari ST that boasts dozens of features for the writer. It was designed by three writers to incorporate features that they wanted in a wordprocessor—the result is a superior package that suits the needs of all ST owners.

TextPro combines its "extra" features with easy operation, flexibility, and speed—but at a very reasonable price. The two-fingered typist will find **TextPro** to be a friendly, user-oriented program, with all the capabilities needed for fine writing and good-looking printouts. **Textpro** offers full-screen editing with mouse or keyboard shortcuts, as well as high-speed input, scrolling and editing. **TextPro** includes a number of easy to use formatting commands, fast and practical cursor positioning and multiple text styles.

Two of **TextPro**'s advanced features are automatic table of contents generation and index generation —capabilities usually found only on wordprocessing packages costing hundreds of dollars. **TextPro** can also print text horizontally (normal typewriter mode) or vertically (sideways). For that professional newsletter look, **TextPro** can print the text in columns—up to six columns per page in sideways mode.

The user can write form letters using the convenient Mail Merge option. **TextPro** also supports GEM-oriented fonts and type styles—text can be **bold**, underlined, *italic*, superscript, ~~outlined~~, etc., and in a number of point sizes. **TextPro** even has advanced features for the programmer for development with its Non-document and C-sourcecode modes.

TextPro ST Features:

- Full screen editing with either mouse or keyboard
- Automatic index generation
- Automatic table of contents generation
- Up to 30 user-defined function keys, max. 160 characters per key
- Lines up to 180 characters using horizontal scrolling
- Automatic hyphenation
- Automatic wordwrap
- Variable number of tab stops
- Multiple-column output (maximum 5 columns)
- Sideways printing on Epson FX and compatibles
- Performs mail merge and document chaining
- Flexible and adaptable printer driver
- Supports RS-232 file transfer (computer-to-computer transfer possible)
- Detailed 65+ page manual

TextPro works with Atari ST systems with one or more single- or double-sided disk drives. Works with either monochrome or color ST monitors.

TexPro allows for flexible printer configurations with most popular dot-matrix printers.

TextPro	Suggested Retail Price: **$49.95**

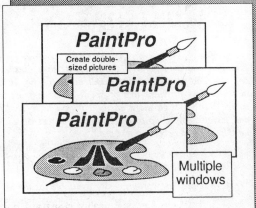
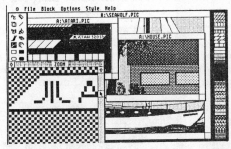
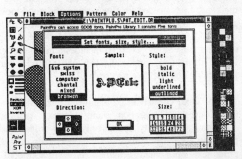
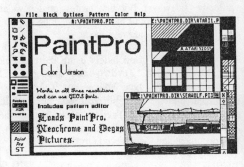

Chartpak ST

Professional-quality charts and graphs on the Atari ST

In the past few years, Roy Wainwright has earned a deserved reputation as a topnotch software author. **Chartpak ST** may well be his best work yet. **Chartpak ST** combines the features of his **Chartpak** programs for Commodore computers with the efficiency and power of GEM on the Atari ST.

Chartpak ST is a versatile package for the ST that lets the user make professional quality charts and graphs <u>fast</u>. Since it takes advantage of the ST's GEM functions, **Chartpak ST** combines speed and ease of use that was unimaginable til now.

The user first inputs, saves and recalls his data using **Chartpak ST**'s menus, then defines the data positioning, scaling and labels. **Chartpak ST** also has routines for standard deviation, least squares and averaging if they are needed. Then, with a single command, your chart is drawn instantly in any of 8 different formats—and the user can change the format or resize it immediately to draw a different type of chart.

In addition to direct data input, **Chartpak ST** interfaces with ST spreadsheet programs spreadsheet programs (such as **PowerLedger ST**). Artwork can be imported from **PaintPro ST** or DEGAS. Hardcopy of the finshed graphic can be sent most dot-matrix printers. The results on both screen and paper are documents of truly professional quality.

Your customers will be amazed by the versatile, powerful graphing and charting capabilities of **Chartpak ST** .

Chartpak ST works with Atari ST systems with one or more single- or double-sided disk drives. Works with either monochrome or color ST monitors. Works with most popular dot-matrix printers (optional).

Chartpak ST   Suggested Retail Price: **$49.95**

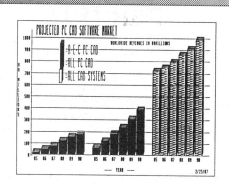

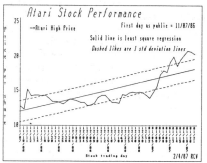

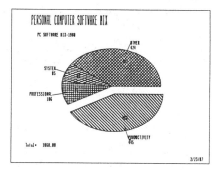

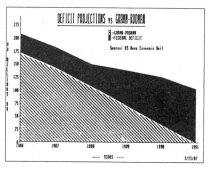

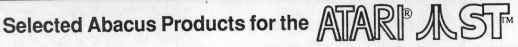

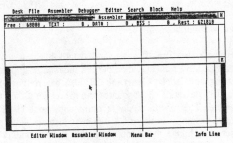